D1569718

The Guided Reinvention
of Language

The Guided Reinvention of Language

ANDREW LOCK
*Department of Psychology, University of Lancaster,
Lancaster, England*

1980

ACADEMIC PRESS

A Subsidiary of Harcourt Brace Jovanovich, Publishers
London   New York   Toronto   Sydney   San Francisco

ACADEMIC PRESS INC. (LONDON) LTD
24/28 Oval Road
London NW1

U.S. Edition published by
ACADEMIC PRESS INC.
111 Fifth Avenue
New York
New York 10003

British Library Cataloguing in Publication Data

Lock, Andrew
  The guided reinvention of language.
  1. Children – Language
  2. Mother and child
  401'.9   LB1139.L3   79-41518

ISBN 0-12-453950-5

Printed in Great Britain by
W. & G. Baird Ltd., at the Greystone Press, Antrim.

Preface

This book is concerned with the earliest phases of a child's development of communication and language. It is, however, not an orthodox book, but a conjectural one. Historically the study of child language has oscillated, shifting periodically from the weltanschauung of linguistics to that of psychology. These shifts occur because the approach of one discipline fails at some point, and a view arising in the other appears to give more hope. But, almost invariably, the shifts have occurred through the poaching of theories that were never originally conceived with the study of child language in mind. Learning theory, for example, was to do with learning, but when applied to language was found lacking, and a turn was made to grammatical theory. This, while concerned with language, has little to offer with regard to developmental questions. Developmental psychology, in turn, is about development, but largely in the context of cognition—of which language is a part, but certainly not the whole—in the individual, with little or no emphasis upon the role of communication in the process.

Here I set myself firmly in that school of thought which sees communication as central to human development and human action: central to both language and cognition. Both of these phenomena are seen as rooted in the social process: both as being constituted through our immersion in, and communication with, our socio-cultural worlds. I have tried to draw from this view a developmental perspective. In doing so I have not committed myself beforehand to any one theoretical paradigm, but have drawn from a variety of linguists, psychologists, philosophers, sociologists and anthropologists whenever I have found them putting forward an insight that seems valuable—sometimes irrespective of the way they have developed those insights themselves. And thus, this is a conjectural book.

Further, not only is it conjectural, but it is intended to promote conjecture. I believe that at this early stage in developmental science any item of its literature will be at best 90% wrong. This item is certainly no exception, and yet even with the sceptical eye of an author I still find it useful: as Jackson Brown sings "I may not have the answer, but I think I've got a plan". It is still making me think, and I hope that, despite its shortcomings, it may spark off ideas in its audience.

Each chapter is written to stand on its own. This means that if the whole book is read it will appear repetitive. It is, though, possible to take just the topics one is interested in and see them in the context of the main arguments without having to spend time going through apparently less relevant chapters.

There are two recent studies on this phase of early language development that need mention here. The first is Greenfield and Smith (1976) *The Structure of Communication in Early Language Development.* I was fortunate to receive from Patricia Greenfield in 1973 the whole of the data corpus on which their book is based, and it will be apparent that I have drawn on both their data and views quite extensively in the later chapters. While often I have offered alternative analyses, and disputed some of their views, I must make it clear that I am in no way trying to denigrate their work. My criticisms are mostly of an immanent nature: I intend in no way to add to the many, and in my view generally unfair, notices their work has received. Their study is closer to the nature and spirit of child language studies than that of many of their critics, and it is most valuable, despite being 90% wrong! Another 90% book is one that bears some remarkable similarities in tone and approach to this one, and yet I have barely mentioned it: Elizabeth Bates' (1976) *Language and Context.* Bates' book covers much the same territory as this, and paints a very similar picture. The difference between them is their emphasis upon the social processes involved in development and the relation between these and Piagetian theory. Whether there can be a direct synthesis between the cognitive and social approaches is a question I have not addressed here: and that is why I have ignored Bates' work. So here I must redress the balance: her book is essential reading for anyone concerned with the study of language development.

The manuscript of the book has gone through a number of changes and revisions over quite a long period of time, and three people in particular have played a major part in assisting its evolution. It began as a Ph.D. thesis, and my supervisor, Chris Singleton, performed the unenviable task of translating many of my gothic constructions into something more like English. It was examined for a Ph.D by John Newson who came to the exam armed with as many written comments as there were pages in the thesis, and proceeded to use them to frighten me to death. His comments have proved a most valuable source for me ever since, and I apologize to him for the number that I have apparently ignored in this final version.

Thirdly, John Shotter. John has been of so much help and inspiration to me that it is difficult to know where to begin thanking him. He was my tutor during the doldrums of a mis-spent undergraduate career. I went to him for my weekly sessions in a state of alienated reluctance for which he provided the antidote by keeping me captive for two hours and thinking aloud at me. Finally I stopped believing that a Turing machine was some kind of bicycle and slowly began to get a glimmering of the question he was pointing to: "what is it to be human?" Since then he has developed his work in a number of papers and books that have gained him international recognition. To have been privy, in a peculiar way, to the early formulations of a brilliant mind is the biggest stroke of luck I have ever had. Since then he has been of constant assistance to me. His influence will be apparent in the content of this book; it is also there in its form. He played a major role in the rewriting and editing of the manuscript into its final form. John must take most of any credit, while I must take all of the blame.

To express my gratitude to everyone who has played a part in keeping me going during the writing could take forever, so those I do not mention should not feel they were not appreciated.

I have benefited greatly from discussions with Roger Clark, Alison Macrae, Paul Harris and Paul Heelas. Jeff Pink did a marvellous job of producing the drawings from video-tape. Keith Brooker and Judith Dyson did a lot to maintain my sanity. But it is to my wife and our respective families that the greatest debt is owed. I am more than aware of the sacrifices they have made to allow me to continue selfishly with academic pursuits, and that I cannot repay them. Thank you.

Not least, there are three mothers and babies who allowed me into their lives. Without them . . . . Finally, my gratitude to the lady who typed most of the manuscript, Sylvia Sumner. I cannot imagine a better typist in skill, cheerfulness and efficiency.

November 1979   ANDREW LOCK
Lancaster

Contents

Acknowledgements

The author and publisher wish to thank the following for their kind permission to reproduce material from other volumes:

Routledge & Kegan Paul Books Ltd. and W. W. Norton & Co. Inc. for quotations from "Play, Dreams and Imitation in Childhood" by Jean Piaget; Routledge & Kegan Paul Books Ltd. and International Universities Press for quotations from "The Origin of Intelligence in the Child" by Jean Piaget; quotations reprinted by permission of Penguin Books Ltd. from *The Biological and the Social* by Martin Richards in Nigel Armistead (ed.) "Reconstructing Social Psychology" (Penguin Education, 1974), p. 236, Copyright© Nigel Armistead and contributors, 1974, and quotations from Aaron V. Cicourel: "Cognitive Sociology" (Penguin Education, 1973), pp. 30, 58, Copyright© Aaron V. Cicourel, 1973; Cambridge University Press for quotations from chapters by J. Shotter, M. Richards and J. Ryan in "The Integration of a Child into a Social World" edited by M. Richards; quotations reprinted from "Mind, Self and Society" by George Herbert Mead by permission of The University of Chicago Press, Copyright © University of 1934 Chicago Press; John Wiley & Sons Inc. for quotations from "Carmichael's Manual of Child Psychology", pp. 335, 336, edited by P. H. Mussen; MIT Press for quotations from "Thought and Language" by L. S. Vygotsky; quotations by permission of the Oxford University Press from "Divinity and Experience" by Godfrey Lienhardt © Oxford University Press 1961, and from "Objective

Knowledge" by Karl Popper © Oxford University Press 1972; George Allen & Unwin (Publishers) Ltd. for quotations from "A First Language" by R. Brown.

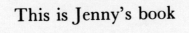
This is Jenny's book

1. Introduction

Whilst there are a number of separately identifiable theories of language development, they all essentially fall into one of two camps. On the one hand there are the nativist theories (for example, Chomsky, 1957 *eg seq*.; Fillmore, 1968) in which the attempt to account for the underlying structural properties of language is made by an appeal to innate properties of organization. On the other are empiricist theories (for example Sampson, 1978; Skinner, 1957) which make the attempt by appealing to the structured nature of the environment as the agent which imposes its organization upon an originally blank perceptual slate. Even though these theories are in fundamental opposition they do share a common emphasis of individualism: of taking a "prisoner in the cell" view that the problem of language development is one faced by, and eventually solved by, a social isolate who must rely solely upon his own intelligence to gain a grip on the nature of the world.

Here, instead, I will advance a much more socially-oriented perspective. Rather than viewing the individual relying on his own abilities, I will approach the problem of language development as one in which he relies to a great extent upon the abilities already developed by others, abilities which are transmitted to him through the process of social interaction. The essential question being asked throughout is this: *How does the child, through interaction with his mother, come to invent and use language?* The characterization that will be given to the emergence of language is that it arises through a process of *guided reinvention*. The perspective taken is not one in which the individual is seen as responsible for developing strategies on his own for the acquisition of knowledge, but one in which those strategies are *transmitted* to him through his interactions *with those who are already in possession of them.*

1.1 The social context of development

The child's development, then, is fundamentally influenced by his mother or caretaker acting towards him on the basis of her perception of what he is trying to do. This influence has three main effects. Firstly, it inducts the child into the specific social world he has been born into. Secondly, it brings him to an agreed and socially shared perception of that world. And thus, thirdly, it also creates the meanings for his actions that will underlie his later development of language. To expand these points, Shotter (1974a: 226) relying heavily on MacMurray (1961: 48) puts the case that:

> the most obvious fact about the human baby is his total helplessness. As MacMurray (1961) puts it, he seems to be "adapted", to speak paradoxically, to being unadapted; he is adapted to complete dependence upon an adult human being. He is born into a love relationship which is inherently personal; he must be treated as if he were a person who could intend purposes; he cannot think for himself, yet he cannot live without thought, so some way must be found of having his thinking done for him. Until he has constructed his own thought mechanisms, I shall propose that he *uses* his mother as a "mechanism" to do the thinking required in the realisation of his intentions.

Thus by living through the mother, the child is an integral part of the adult world. Spitz (1965) uses the very graphic term of "psychological symbiosis" to describe this relationship. The process of development then comes to be seen as one of a transition from personal dependence to independence, a taking over by the individual child of the functions the mother initially performs for him, a moving away from symbiosis. The child "cannot, even theoretically, live an isolated existence; he is not an independent individual . . . . Only in the process of development does he learn to achieve a relative independence and that only by *appropriating the techniques of a rational social tradition*" (MacMurray, 1961: 50; my italics). Now, as Shotter (1974a, p. 223) notes:

> from all this it follows that a baby is not a machine although he may be said to possess mechanisms; nor an animal although in some respects he may be said to function organically; if he is to develop as an individual

personality he must be treated as a full term in a personal relationship as a being amenable to rationality.

It is in this fundamental way that the field of social interaction becomes essential to the developmental perspective. The child functions as part of the adult world from birth, and his development is one in which he wrests his mental operations away from his mother, appropriates them to himself, to *become* an individual; and those operations only exist as part of a rational social tradition. The crucial process in this transition of his abilities from his mother to himself is the act of communication.

1.2 Communicative acts

The majority of contemporary investigations into language development have adopted either the "proposition" or the "sentence" as key theoretical concepts. Linguistic theories, which provided the original impetus for these studies, are, after all, concerned with the analysis of sentences and propositions. Bloom (1973), however, has provided many reasons why the indiscriminate use of these notions in child language studies is unwarranted.

In addition to the reasons she advances a further one will be put forward later as a central point: that propositions, and hence sentences do not really exist at all in early child language and its forebears, but only have an *implicit* existence. Hence, they are not directly applicable to the analysis of child language. But the inapplicability of these two concepts creates something of a vacuum. Some anchoring concept is necessary to allow apparently distinct actual performances to be counted as equivalent. This concept can be neither of those noted above, if only because they are too narrow to encompass all the relevant "performances". Similarly the concept of "the social act", stemming from Mead's writings (see Chapter 3) is inapplicable, but this time because it encompasses too many events. Again, Searle's (1969) conception of "the speech act" is not ideal in cases prior to the child's possessing speech, because what is meant by saying that the child can perform "speech acts" before he has speech is unclear.

The concept of "acts" implicit in these paradigms has its attractions, for acts are

> not to be identified either with the actions needed to perform them, nor with the movements involved in the action. There are many different

ways in which the same act may be performed. All have the same meaning through their identity with respect to the act of which they are a performance.   (Harré and Secord, 1972: 11)

Hence the notion of *communicative act* will be adopted. A subdivision of this generic category is necessary: firstly, into the true *communicative act* in which the "sender" *intends* to communicate with another: and secondly, the unintended, but none the less effective, *perceived communicative act*, in which the "recipient" perceives a communicative act where the "sender" does not intend one. Thus actions on the part of the infant which are not performed by him with the intention of communicating, but which are acted upon by an adult human agent *as if* they were part of an intended communicative act, fall under this second category of the perceived communicative act. A further advantage of this differentiation is that instances of true *communicative* acts are capable of being integrated with work already conducted into the development of *speech* acts (e.g. Dore, 1975), since speech acts can be seen as a subcategory within the communicative act.

Before going any further the question as to how to represent the meaning conveyed in a communicative act, a meaning which may well be only implicit and unstated, must be dealt with. To do this I am going to take Sanborn's suggestion (1971: 84) that the development of language be looked at from the *"genetico- historical standpoint with adult speech as the end development"*. Now, in performing a perceived communicative act the child has his actions reflected back to him by his mother as meaningful, and the meanings they are afforded are the same as those conveyed by certain linguistic utterances. Crying, for example, may come to possess the same meaning for the child as "I want . . .", with whatever he wants being supplied by the context in which he cries. Consequently, I am going to represent the meanings of communicative acts by linguistic glosses from the language the child is being inducted into.

Basing the unit of analysis in the act of communication is not only convenient, but allows a wide range of phenomena to be included in a description of any eventual grammer the child might exhibit. Recent linguistic formulations of grammars have tied themselves closely to purely linguistic components, with the result, as Lakoff (1972: 90) points out, that:

> there are areas of linguistic competence that cannot be described in any
> theory that does not allow an integration of information about the context

in which the discourse takes place ... and the purely linguistically relevant information the sentence seeks to convey: superficial syntax, choice of lexical items, and semantics aside from contextually relevant meaning elements.

But by adopting the communicative act these problems can be overcome. *Any communicative act is comprised of two components: firstly the actions that are performed; and secondly the situational context in which their performance occurs.* This is represented in Fig. 1.1.

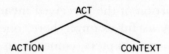

Fig. 1.1. The components of an act.

Meanings can be represented within this framework: as an example, consider a child's crying. The action of crying by the very young infant constitutes a perceived communicative act, and is perceived by the mother as meaning *I want something.* This meaning is *constructed* by the mother out of the influence of the action of crying within the context in which it occurs. Both the action and the context "carry" part of this constructed meaning: the cry "carrying" the relationship between the child and the object implicated by his crying. For example, if the child cries say four hours after his last feed it is likely that his crying will be perceived as indicating hunger—crying "expresses the need" and the context determines it. This is shown diagrammatically, in Fig. 1.2.

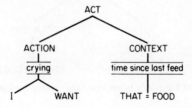

Fig. 1.2. The meaning conveyed by the components of the act of crying.

Additional factors can be included in these diagrammatic representations. If the message *I want food* is the interpretation given by the mother to her infant's crying, but is not intended by the infant to have this meaning, then the meanings of the act are enclosed in brackets (see Fig. 1.3).

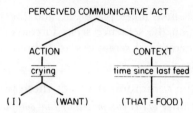

Fig. 1.3. Representation of crying as a perceived communicative act.

If, however, the action is used by the infant with some knowledge at its root, then that portion of the perceived meaning which his action conveys is italized. A useful example here, one which is frequently referred to in subsequent chapters, comes from Piaget (1951: 60):

> Laurent . . . between 0;3(15) and 0;4 reacts to visual signals. When, after being dressed as usual just before the meal, he is put in my arms in position for nursing, he looks at me and then searches all around, looks at me again, etc.—but he does not attempt to nurse. When I place him in his mother's arms without his touching the breast, he looks at her and immediately opens his mouth wide, cries, moves about, in short reacts in a completely significant way.

Laurent here uses his crying with knowledge: crying makes *want* determinate in the perceived meaning of his activity, yet all other aspects of that meaning are determined by contextual features. Laurent's behaviour is illustrated in Fig. 1.4.

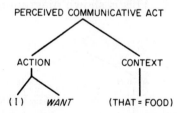

Fig. 1.4. Representation of Laurent's behaviour (as reported by Piaget, 1951).

Similarly, reaching towards an object, which may occur in many different contexts and with differing intentions, can constitute a perceived communicative act. In this case, however, the meaning is made determinate in a different way to instances involving crying, as shown in Fig. 1.5. This mode of presentation is used extensively hereafter: its usefulness will then become more apparent, as will that of the ploy of representing the child's implied meanings in terms of adult words, a

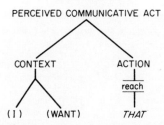

Fig. 1.5. Representation of reaching as a perceived communicative act.

tactic justified by the adoption of Sanborn's suggestion (1971) noted earlier. On occasions, however, a shorthand representation is used— merely the bottom line of these diagrams. Laurent's behaviour, for example, would be given as (I) *WANT* (THAT). No distinction is shown in these shorthand forms between perceived and intended communicative acts. In practice, this does not present any great difficulties. The representation of the child's implied meanings is discussed further in Chapter 5.

A final point here concerns conventions that are adopted with respect to these shorthand representations when they are used to represent forces underlying linguistic utterances. Often a child will use a word to refer to some aspect of a situation where he could have used an alternative word to refer to another aspect of the same situation. Suppose, for example, the child can refer to both the change in state of an object undergoing some action, and the object undergoing that action. In the first case we have a semantic force (see Chapter 5) given as, say (THAT OBJECT) (IS GOING) *DOWN*: in the second *CUP* (IS GOING) (DOWN). To these two instances a common semantic force may be given:

$$X_o \text{ (IS CHANGING STATE) } X_s$$

Here subscripts are used to delineate the general symbol X as an instance of an object, X_o, a state or change in state, X_s, or an action, X_a. Further, a dotted line under an element in the force so represented indicates that the production of that element is optional. Thus, in the example given, a semantic force is being represented that underlies a number of different utterances: X_o (IS CHANGING STATE) X_s underlies both the single-word utterances *cup* and *down* in the uses mentioned above.

2. An outline of Peter's language development

In this chapter the general outline of language development I am suggesting is reviewed through observations of one child, Peter. This outline indicates a sequence of developmental stages: the development of actions which function communicatively through the mother's perception of them; the metamorphosis of these to the status of communicative gestures, in which the child realizes the communicative function of his action and employs them for this purpose; the combination of gestures—initially they are used singly, then they are used together; the emergence of referential words; and finally the use of words in combination with the child's previously developed gestures. This outline is then expanded and given a more detailed treatment in the subsequent chapters.

Observation 1
Peter; age 7 (23) (i.e. seven months and twenty-three days): Peter's play with his toys consists of holding them at arm's length and waving his arms about, sometimes clapping his hands together, sometimes banging them onto his chest, sometimes banging them on the floor, etc. It is only with new objects that he reverts to placing them primarily in his mouth.

Observation 2
Peter; age 8 (9): Peter is playing with a piece of cellophane by waving it about, as usual, and concurrently "lalling" to himself. In the course of his play he bangs his chest, and in doing so causes a hiccup in his lalling. He immediately

stops and looks about, and then recreates a hiccup in the same fashion. The next few minutes of his playing consist of banging his chest to make quick, successive chains of hiccups, then waving his arms wildly, then banging his chest again. Later the same day he repeats this, without having a toy in his hand. This schema becomes one of his standard ways of exploring new toys, and a standard form of amusement when he has none.

There can be seen in the transition between these observations the chance discovery by Peter of what, in Piagetian terminology, constitutes a procedure to make interesting sights or events last (Piaget, 1952: 201). In the course of exercising an established schema, Peter retroactively discovers a new goal to which those actions can be put: in pursuing an usual mode of play he discovers a novelty—that he can use his arm-waving to make "interesting" noises. Now,

> Consider the act of randomly waving my hand in the air . . . . Now suppose that, in this random thrashing about, I happen to touch something, and that this satisfies and thereby makes partially determinate a need, a need to cope with things. I can then repeat *whatever I did*—this time *in order to* repeat something—without appealing to the laws necessary to describe it as a physical motion. I now have a way of bringing two objects together in objective space without appealing to any principle except "Do that again".   (Dreyfus, 1967: 28)

Here Peter has retroactively realized the principle of "Do that again": his arm-waving has come to be used as an active attempt to reconstitute an event, and in this case the event happens to be contingent upon his actions.

Observation 3
Peter; age 8 (16): Peter is sitting on the floor and I am in front of him, snapping my fingers, first to his left, then to his right and so on. He will visually attend to these events, looking from side to side, but does not show any anticipation. When I stop, he looks straight at me and waves his arms as though he were going to bang his chest. I then snap my fingers again and the sequence continues. I then switch to building a tower within his reach out of some blocks. He knocks this down and immediately looks at me, laughs and waves his arms in the same way as above, until I rebuild the tower, whereupon he knocks it down again. The sequence thus continues in this manner. If I do not rebuild the tower Peter stops waving and continues looking at me and then resumes his arm-waving with great vigour.

Here Peter proceeds to exercise arm-waving to *recreate an event* (not merely to make hiccups), and as it happens these events are not directly contingent upon his actions. His arm-waving appears to be

> an attempt to preserve the spectacle through action at a distance . . . .
> Such procedures are of course irrational only from the standpoint of an
> observer familiar with the causal texture of the environment; for the
> infant they simply constitute an *altogether natural generalisation* from previ-
> ous secondary circular reaction experiences.
>
> (Flavell, 1963: 106; my italics)

Piaget notes that his own son developed an arm-waving procedure for the purpose of making interesting sights last. From a specific beginning, these schemata came to have a perceived general efficacy—being applied in a variety of circumstances.

> It therefore seems apparant that the movement of shaking the arm, at first
> inserted in a circular schema of the whole, has been removed from its
> context to be used, more and more frequently, as a "procedure" to make
> any interesting spectacle last.   (Piaget, 1952: 201, obs. 115)

This is true of Peter's arm-waving, but if Observation 4 is further taken into account, it becomes apparent that there is no communicative intent behind his actions:

Observation 4
Peter; age 8 (16): The draught from an open door causes some letters to fall off the mantlepiece. Peter looks at them, laughs and waves his arms.

His arm-waving is aimed at an occurrence in an attempt to recreate it, and does not go beyond this. However, not all the events he aims his schema at are contingent upon his actions. In Observation 3, *it is only because I am able to construe* Peter's actions *as being equivalent* to the meaning "Do that again" that I am able to make those actions effective. I possess the power of agency such that I *can* "Do that again", whereas those things that do not have this power, nor the ability to construe his actions as meaningful, will remain unsusceptible to his schema.

In perceiving Peter's actions in a particular way I create them as *communicative* actions. For Peter to become able to use these actions for communication he must come to see them in the same way as I do; we must both agree upon their value. The creation of this agreed value for Peter's schema, so that he may use it deliberately for communication, appears to occur quite naturally and as a result of a spontaneous reorganization of the child's schema on the basis of its prior uses and effects.

Observation 5

Peter; age 8 (19): (a) I am banging a margarine jar on the floor within Peter's field of vision. Between bangs Peter waves his arms and laughs, and so I continue to do it—much to his evident delight. When the jar comes within his reach he takes it from me and bangs it himself, with much laughter. (b) For an unknown reason a glass tumbler on the table starts to crack, making a loud noise each time the crack enlarges. The noises attract Peter's attention and he eventually locates their source. He looks at the glass and laughs, but does not wave his arms.

While drawing positive inferences from the non-occurrence of an event is, at best, a dubious affair, from this time onward Peter was not observed to use his arm-waving for the recreation of an event in which there was no agent to appeal to. There were, however, occasions on which he would wave his arms in the presence of an agent when the event that had occurred had not been created by that agent; for example, if he knocked down a pile of bricks while playing on his own he would laugh and wave his arms. He will produce his schema for preserving and repeating events that I, his mother or father, or he himself, make happen, but not, apparently, for fortuitous events where there is no agent to appeal to for the reconstitution of the event. In this manner his "altogether natural generalisation" has become refined, in an altogether natural way.

Even with this distinction in his behaviour usage, however, there is no need to postulate any communicative intent to his actions: he may merely be making a distinction among various classes of events, only some of which he perceives as recreatable. But in Observations 3 and 5, while he is not waving his arms with the intention of communicating, only to make something happen again, I can treat his actions *"as if" he were communicating*; and on the basis of this "as if" I am able to fulfil his intention of recreating an event. I treat Peter's actions as an appeal to me to "Do that again". From the communicative point of view this

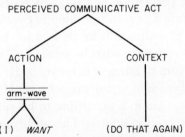

Fig. 2.1. The meaning conveyed by arm-waving, Observations 3 and 5.

particular episode in which both Peter and I are implicated may be given the structure shown in Fig. 2.1.

Observation 6
Peter; age 8 (21): Peter is on the floor with many of his toys, and I am sitting with him. His attention is focused on removing all his building blocks from their receptacle. He grasps a block, a fairly hit-and-miss affair, and without looking lifts it over the edge of the box and drops it on the floor. He immediately brings his hand back to "grasp" another block; this he continues till the box is empty and all the blocks are strewn on the floor. He then turns to me and waves his arms. I pick up a brick and give it to him, but he does not take it, and he continues waving his arms. I put the brick down on top of another one, and Peter laughs and waves his arms more vigorously. I then build up a tower of five blocks which Peter knocks over, laughs, looks at me and waves his arms again. I rebuild the tower and so the game continues.

While Peter's use of his arm-waving again constitutes an "altogether natural generalisation" in that it is being used in a context in which it has previously been successful, there is here an important addition: it is not initially used to recreate an immediately prior occurrence. The first use of his arm-waving in this observation appears to have been *in order to start* what for Peter is an "enjoyable" game. All the ingredients of Observation 3 are present at the outset of this sequence bar one: the bricks are scattered on the floor and I am in front of him, but there has been no tower built or knocked down. I am none the less able to perceive his actions with a similar value, but with a "referential" difference; I perceive him as communicating *I want (do that again)* with, in the first instance *that* referring to "the prior event", and in the second to "the game". Peter has become capable of anticipating what might happen; he is able to perceive the situation he creates in Observation 6 with values that have become established through my earlier games with him, and "tower-bashing" has been the most common of these. On the basis of this perception he can use a portion of his behaviour, now seemingly having a negotiated value between us, to actualize the anticipated event. The situation he creates for himself is sufficiently structured for him to perceive what he wants, and the event sufficiently significant to allow him to attempt to create it. He can now initiate the game; he is not dependent upon my whims. He can recognize the situation he is in, and act in it according to his retroactively acquired values, rather than merely react to it. This ability generalizes, so that he becomes able to use this schema in other contexts.

Observation 7
Peter; age 8 (28): Peter is being fed, but towards the end of the meal he is no longer looking at the spoon, but at his bottle of orange-juice which is nearby on the floor, and he waves his arms at the same time. Mother: "Look, just two more spoonfuls and then you can have a drink", and she attempts to pursue this intention. Peter keeps on arm-waving and refuses to eat, and so mother gives him a drink. He then finishes off his meal.

In this case the employment of the schema has subtly changed again. Its previous usage to make something happen in isolation from the immediate past (Observation 6) was still within the context of a situation in which it had already been used successfully. Here there is neither an event to be repeated nor a "game" to be reactivated, just something that is wanted. This aspect is also immediately apparent in Observation 8.

Observation 8
Peter; age 9 (16): Peter is sitting on the floor playing with a football, and I am seated some eight feet from him reading a newspaper. He starts crying and I look across to him. He looks at me and waves his arms, then looks across to his football which has rolled away, out of his reach. I retrieve it for him and he continues to play with it quietly.

It is noticeable now that Peter's usage of his schema has moved by a series of "altogether natural generalisations" from the restrictive idiosyncratic value of "Do that again" to the more open and shared "I want that . . . ", where the arm-waving indicates that he wants something, and the context in which he acts determines for his "listener" what that something actually is. Peter has thus come to realize the potential latencies of the situations in which he has acted. Such acts of intentional communication may be given the structure shown in Fig. 2.2.

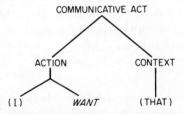

Fig. 2.2. Act-structure within which arm-raising may be used for intentional communication, cf. Observation 9.

Parenthetically, it may be noted that crying in Observation 8 is unlikely to be either intentional or communicative in nature. Peter's crying is not aimed at attracting my attention, for the purpose of then communicating by arm-waving, but is apparently a reflex expression of his frustration at not being able to retrieve his football—he does not crawl at this time. However, his arm-waving can only function communicatively if he has my attention, owing to its existence within the visual dimension alone. Here he has obtained my attention fortuitously; later, however, he develops strategies to obtain another's attention intentionally by the use of vestigial crying.

Returning to Dreyfus' analysis (1967): initially Peter happened upon an action that seemingly enabled him to satisfy, and currently make partially determinate a "need"—he can then repeat whatever he did to repeat the effects. Secondly, he can then use his actions in an attempt to preserve or reconstitute immediately prior events—"an altogether natural generalisation"—and where he is successful he is able to satisfy his semi-determinate specific "need". Finally, through another series of-effective "natural generalisations" he can repeat whatever he did *in order* to satisfy *any* need. The latter usage has the effect of further determining these needs and making their communicative expression more determinate at the same time (see Chapter 3 on this point).

Up to this time Peter's communicative behaviour is relatively inefficient. His actual behaviour only carries a portion of the total message implicated. His arm-waving possesses the negotiated value "I want", and no more; he does not make determinate by his behaviour what the object of those needs is. Crying is similar: it is obvious to us as adults that the crying child "wants" something, but his actions give little indication of what that something might be. In such cases it is the context in which the actions are produced that makes the message completely determinate. To make the object of his communication determinate the child must develop further communicative actions.

In the next series of observations attention is focused on this second aspect of Peter's development of communicative strategies: not on the expression and later communication of a state of need, but on the indicating of *what* it is that is wanted.

Observation 9
Peter; age 9 (17): Mother is playing with Peter. He stops what he is doing and reaches out to his right toward his toy dog. It is beyond his reach, but mother leans over and gives it to him.

Observation 10
Peter; age 9 (12)–10 (7): Similar instances of the above joint activity (Observation 9) occur regularly through this period. Peter reaches towards objects beyond his grasp and if anyone is paying attention to him he is given that object. Reaching here involves not just extending the arm, but a straining of the whole body in the direction of the desired object.

Peter would strain to reach an object to the extent of falling flat on his face from a sitting position. He made no direct attempt to attract anyone's attention, thus indicating the communicative intent of his action to be nil, but was continually successful in attracting attention because of the loud sounds of exertion he produced, or by cries of frustration when he was unsuccessful. It is interesting that cries of frustration always occurred when the child was still stretching towards the object: he never relaxed and then cried. Basically, then, his actions must be viewed as part of a direct attempt to obtain an object—not being in any way deliberately communicative.

Observation 11
Peter; age 10 (17): Peter's reaching for objects has now become stylized. There is no longer obvious total body orientation and straining toward the object, but solely the raising of the arm, to be held in an outstretched position towards the object. For example: Peter is playing, but he leaves his toys and crawls to the fireplace. He pulls himself up erect by grasping the gas-fire and looks around. He then strains toward his orange-juice beaker which he has just seen. It is beyond his reach. He turns from the fire and meets me in eye contact. Maintaining this he lifts his arm in the direction of the beaker. As I get up he turns back to the beaker and takes it when I give it to him. He drinks from it.

During the period covered by these observations Peter's reaching action has changed. The action which conveys his intention has been modified by the response it gains from results, culminating in his using a stylized version of the action to effect his intention. The action of reaching has been created as a social object from his behaviour, such that it has a value which has been established by active agreement common to both Peter and his mother: they both perceive it in the same way— "Give me what I reach for". He can now effectively point.

During this period, Peter has become an efficient crawler. Consequently he seldom "asks" for things if he is able to reach them by himself. His communications now appear to fall into three categories:

(1) During play situations when something "pleases" him he waves his arms, with the result that the event is reconstituted for him.

(2) Again in play situations, when he is apparently unwilling to crawl for something within easy reach, he points at it.

(3) When objects he wants are outside the world encompassed by his crawling he again points, e.g. for a toy on the table. Thus, at this time, his arm-waving reverts back to its original function, and pointing takes its place for the communication of needs.

However, from a structural point of view, pointing differs with respect to arm-waving as shown in Fig. 2.3. With pointing he is now singling

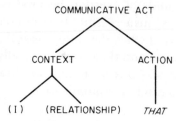

Fig. 2.3. Act-structure of communicative pointing.

out part of the environment, but leaves the context in which he acts, and which he effectively creates by acting, to make communicatively determine why that part of the environment has been singled out. It is important to note this point, because once Peter has developed the pointing gesture, he does not solely use it with the value "I want that":

Observation 12
Peter, age 11 (5): I am holding Peter up to look out of the window. As a car goes past in the road Peter watches it and points at it.

This aspect of pointing—singling out objects demonstratively—becomes of great importance, but because of their two different functions acts of pointing create certain "interpretive" problems as well (see below).

Thus far it has been possible to trace the development of two distinct communicative actions. The first of these emerged from a relatively restricted usage into a global one, only to revert as the second develops and comes to prominence. The second of these develops for use in one form of act and then diverges to be used for another purpose as well. It is often the case that the contextual information surrounding the employment of pointing is insufficient to enable an observer to distinguish between these two uses. At around the age of one year Peter's pointing is often used within the framework of "referential" communication games—primarily that of object-labelling play. This "game" occurs very often and consists, in this case, of pointing at an object and exclaiming "der". It soon becomes apparent that Peter *does not* want the object he has singled out, and thus his pointing at things when he *does* want them becomes ineffective, as his mother cannot readily discriminate between the two different uses and the differing intentions behind them. Peter's eventual response to this state of affairs is to revert to arm-waving as a means of indicating he wants something, and using it *in conjunction with* pointing:

Observation 13
Peter; age 13 (13): Peter points at his toy dog on the table and says "der".
Mother: That's a dog.
He then immediately points to the television and says "der".
Mother: No, silly, that's the television.

Observation 14
Peter; age 13 (13): Peter and his mother are in eye contact. Peter waves his arms and points to the dog on the table and says "der". His mother passes it down to him.

By using arm-waving in conjunction with pointing he distinguishes for the addresses whether the action is meant as part of a game or "seriously". Arm-waving is used again as it was structured in Fig. 2.1 but this time it is in conjunction with pointing as structured in Figs 2.2 and 2.3. These two abilities have functionally coalesced to yield that shown in Fig. 2.4. With such an ability it is clear that a greater proportion of communicative determination lies within Peter's behaviour than previously. His communication is not entirely independent of the context of its production, since the desired object has to be present in the environment to complete the act of pointing.

Observation 15
Peter; age 14 (4): Peter has acquired the word "darg" which refers to his toy dog, real dogs, dogs heard barking outside, etc. In non-labelling situations his use of it is as follows:
(1) Mother is playing with Peter, getting him to fill a box with all his toys.

B

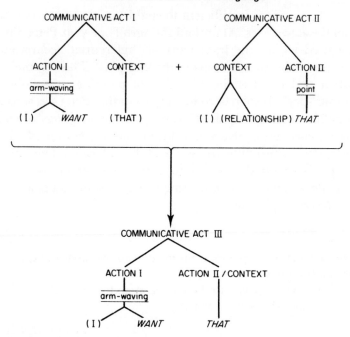

Fig. 2.4. Relation between act-structure of Peter's communicative ability at time of Observation 14 and its antecedents.

Peter gathers every object in reach and puts them in the box. He turns to me (I am about four feet away), looks at the toy dog at my feet, waves his arms and says "darg". I throw it across to him.

(2) Mother empties the box to start the game over again. I retrieve the toy dog. In requesting it this time Peter looks at me, waves his arm, points at the dog with his other arm and says "darg". I give it to him.

As may be seen, Peter's early use of words for communicative purposes is functionally akin to his use of gesture: it may be termed "vocal gesturing". In the same way that the gesture of pointing isolates an object in the environment, so does this vocal gesturing: and at this age Peter's words were only observed to be used in the presence of the object to which they referred. However, vocal gesturing inherently contains greater potentialities than a physical gesture such as pointing; it contains its own reference and does not require complementation by contextual determination. At this stage, however, "darg" is only used if there is a "dog" perceptually present in the environment, and as such the vocal gesture is akin to pointing. Thus, this early use of words may be represented as in Fig. 2.5.

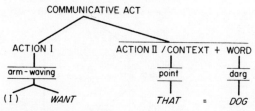

Fig. 2.5. Act-structure of early word–gesture use.

How words came to be used in the absence of their referents requires further study, but Peter quite rapidly attained that ability:

Observation 16
Peter; age 15 (4): Peter says "darg" when there is no external stimulus present: no real or toy dog, no picture, no barking outside. He is sitting in his feeding chair waiting for dinner. Mother leaves the stove and goes out of the kitchen, reappearing a few moments later with the toy dog in her hand. She gives it to Peter.

The mother has acted upon Peter's vocalization even though there was no apparent intention behind it, and thus she takes the effective usage of his behaviour outside the domain of his own competence. She has extended his usage into the realm of symbolization, and given him the chance to exploit voluntarily what he has just accomplished unintentionally: to turn his vocal gestures into true words.

Observation 17
Peter; age 15 (9): Peter is in the bath when he waves his arms and says "darg".
Mother: Not now.
Peter makes it impossible for bathing to continue successfully and repeats his arm-waving and saying of "darg".
Mother: Oh, all right then!
She goes out and returns with the toy dog.
She gives it to Peter, and both he and the dog have a thorough wash.

True word use may be represented as in Fig. 2.6. It should be noted here that with the development of this ability Peter is communicating, *by his own isolated actions* and in a conventionalized manner, something about *the relationship between himself and "darg"*. The demarcation of this relationship is dependent on the structure of this communication, and in this sense his acts may be classed as "structure-dependent" as opposed to "context-dependent".

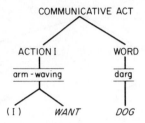

Fig. 2.6. Act-structure of later word–gesture use.

The above sequences trace the development of actions that have undergone changes in the intention with which the child employs them. Peter's arm-waving started with the intention of repeating an interesting event; his pointing with the intention of grasping an object. Both have ended up being used deliberately to convey an intention, and both these intentions are different from the original. In the next sequence of observations the development of another communicative action is discussed, but in contrast with the above, this action has *no* intention behind it to begin with. It is something that the child merely does, and to use it intentionally he has to create that intentional use for it.

It might be argued that in the first sequence, that of arm-waving, the action was initially without intention, and the child only retroactively discovered one. It was, however, from this discovery that the whole sequence became a possibility: in attempting to pursue his intentions in the physical world they become transformed by their relevance in the social world. In this present case, however, the action is not associated with attempts by the child to accomplish any goals whatsoever. The action in question is the "hiccup" noises that Peter created at the time of Observation 2.

This "hiccupping" became detached from the arm-waving schema when Peter discovered that it was possible to make such a noise without physically banging his chest. Since it was his arm-waving that he came to perceive as his "effective action", it might be expected that the hiccup component would die out as this arm-waving became stylized and communicative. However, Peter seemed to have a vested interest in this noise—it was his obvious delight at its discovery that was the starting point for the above sequence, had he not liked the noise he would presumably not have gone to such efforts to recreate it—and the hiccup was preserved and incorporated into his vocal repertoire. Making such noises is dependent upon moving the chest in and out quickly. Peter soon discovered that this chest action could be sustained by breathing shallowly and rapidly, and that the noise could be produced during both in- and exhalation.

This noise maintained no association with the arm-waving schema, but merely became incorporated into his vocal repertoire, becoming his most common utterance. Because it was so common it was produced in numerous situations. Sounds gain their quality from the configuration of the vocal tract; different configurations yielding different sound qualities. Consequently, if Peter "hiccupped" when happy the sound was of a different quality than if it was produced when he was unhappy: these two states exhibit different facial expressions which result in concomitant changes in the configuration of the vocal tract.

By the age of 8 (19) this vocalization had been established as autonomous. At this time Peter's response to situations was of a global nature: if something made him happy he smiled and produced hiccupping laughs; if unhappy he cried, wriggled, and out came crying hiccups. Similarly, if he were "bored" or frustrated, he frowned and grizzled hiccups. For example:

Observation 18
Peter; age 8 (20): I am just about to leave the house and am taking my car-keys from my pocket when I drop them on the floor. Peter is sitting among a pile of toys not paying me any attention. On hearing the noise of the keys he turns towards me. I pick the keys up by the fob and they jangle together. Peter smiles and produces hiccup laughs. I realize what has interested him:
A: No, you can't have them, I've got to go.
I put the keys back in my pocket and walk away. Peter produces violent crying hiccups.

In these situations Peter produces the noise as part of a *general bodily reaction* to events. Because of this the interpretation that can be given to them is very wide. Taking his frustrated or "bored" grizzles as an example, the mother interpreted them in varying situations as: "He's fed up being in his playpen"; "You want to come out don't you?"; "He's getting mad with that toy again—you can't get them in the right holes can you, you want me to do it"; "Oh, is your train stuck, I'll get it out for you". In these cases of frustration it is possible to see a common thread running through the mother's interpretation of Peter's grizzling. She perceives his actions *as if* he were attempting to do something specific and that he is being unsuccessful; she perceives the grizzle as a request for assistance when it undoubtedly is not. She believes Peter is intending to do something, projects herself into the situation she perceives, asks "What could I do in that position?", and acts upon the result of this deliberation. For example:

Observation 19
Peter; age 10 (7): Peter has been completely ignored for about twenty minutes. During this time he has emptied all his building blocks from their container, thrown them all around the room, found a loose end in his jumper and unravelled the sleeve, and explored most of the possibilities of getting tangled up. He has a form-box in his hand and one of the shaped pieces in the other, making no attempt to do anything with them; he is also making loud frustration grizzles, when his mother walks in the room.
Mother: Can't you get those in the holes? Let me help.
She then proceeds to play with him and the toy. Peter becomes interested and the game goes on for five minutes or so.

Observation 20
Peter; age 10 (29): It is now apparent that Peter can play with the form-box and pieces with some understanding of the task. He no longer throws the pieces around, or tries to smash the box apart. Instead he attempts to push the pieces through the holes. Success is largely a matter of chance. He attempts to push a cube through a star-shaped hole. It does not go, and Peter hiccups and grizzles in frustration. Mother intervenes and the problem is overcome.

Observation 21
Peter; age 10 (29): Peter is playing with his pull-along train and gets it stuck among the chair and table legs. He pulls harder and harder on the string but nothing happens. He then pulls and grizzles at the same time. Mother comes in from the kitchen.
Mother: What's the matter now? Oh, is your train stuck? Just a minute, I'll get
         it out now.

In Observations 20 and 21 Peter's frustrated sounds are produced as a *reaction* to his inability to actualize his apparent intention. But this reaction functions within the dyadic situation, implicating an adult just as effectively as if it were in fact a voluntary communicative portion of his behaviour: the characteristics of the sound both alert the mother and inform her that something is amiss. She assumes the grizzling *is* aimed at her, when that really seems unlikely. Eventually, however, these frustration noises are transformed to yield an intentional communicative function:

Observation 22
Peter; age 14 (4): Peter brings me his squeaky ball, gives it to me and grizzles.

Previously when he has done this he has waved his arms and consequently I have pressed the ball to make it squeak. I do the same this time but no noise is forthcoming. Peter takes it back and squeezes it, grizzles and gives it back to me. I squeeze it, and then find that the bit that makes it squeak is missing. A: Oh.
Peter grizzles. I go to his toy-box and eventually find the squeaky bit, which I push back into the ball. Peter has now lost interest and so I leave the ball on the floor. Some minutes later he picks up the ball and squeezes it. It squeaks, he laughs, and then brings it to me, gives it to me and waves his arm. I press it a bit violently and the squeeky bit shoots out. Peter takes it back, laughing and squeezes it. He stops laughing, squeezes it again, hands it back to me and grizzles.

In this case, Peter is using the grizzle not as a reaction to the fact that his intention is frustrated in his attempts to realize it in his actions, but as a gesture aimed at invoking my "help" in pursuing his goal. The grizzling functions in the same way as it did previously, but this time it has a voluntary basis: Peter apparently intends it to function as it does. By treating this sound *as if* it were communicative from the start, the mother has created a value for it congruent with her perceptions. She creates that value *for* Peter's grizzles, and Peter comes to utilize that value in his voluntary behaviour.

In the first sequences of development above, what occurred was the transformation by dyadic action of the intention behind an action: Peter's arm-waving was created as intentional by chance, and interaction with adults resulted in new uses for that action being opened up for him. What he could put to one use he became able to be put to many uses, by a series of altogether natural generalizations on his part as to what the action was *in fact responsible for causing*. In this last series, however, a crucial difference may be seen, in that the ultimate gesture commenced as a non-intentional natural reaction to some state of affairs. But again, its function in interaction—what it was that was contingent upon its production—has likewise become apparent to Peter: he realizes the contingencies his action is responsible for and comes to be able to use this realization in the control of his behaviour.

In the course of this chapter three main events have been dealt with. Firstly, in the arm-waving, pointing and hiccupping sequences the child can be seen exploiting his natural actions by transforming them into a voluntary possession that he can use intentionally. Secondly and concurrently there is the development of his ability to exploit the inherent communicative aspects of his actions: to communicate his needs *and* the object implicated by these needs. Finally, his communication becomes more and more independent of the context of its production. The result of these developments is that the child exhibits a use of behaviour which can be termed language. The following chapters discuss these developments more thoroughly.

3. A theoretical perspective
for language development

3.1 The origins and production of meaningful actions

This chapter outlines the theoretical approach to language development that both results from and underlies this study. I will begin with three complementary points, one coming from the American philosopher G. H. Mead and the other two from the Russian psychologist, L. S. Vygotsky. To take Mead first: he considered the basis of human intelligence to lie within social interaction, within "the adjustment to one another of the acts of different human individuals within the human social process; an adjustment which takes place through communication . . . . The central factor in such adjustment is 'meaning' " (Mead, 1934: 75).

In Mead's view,

> the mechanism of meaning is . . . present in the social act before the emergence of consciousness or awareness of meaning occurs. The act or adjustive response of the second organism gives to the gesture of the first organism the meaning which it has. (Mead, 1934: 77–78)

Meaning thus exists in social interaction, whether or not the interactants whose behavioural adjustments towards each other create that meaning are aware of its existence. It is the *adjustive response* of the other organism that is the *meaning* of the gesture. In sum, Mead's view may be given thus:

(1) *Meaning is objectively present in social interaction, having as its locus the triadic relationship between the gesture, the response of another to it, and the result of the social act so initiated.*

Turning to the points stemming from Vygotsky's work, they can both be seen to have a close relationship to that of Mead's directly above. In his writings, Vygotsky advances two separate formulations of a proposed psychological law. A major concern in his work is the concept of instruction: what the child can first do spontaneously in one context he can later do deliberately in any context after receiving "instruction" from an adult. Thus, intentional action arises through interaction with an adult. Vygotsky's first formulation of this point is in *Thought and Language* (1962: 90):

(2) *In order to subject a function to intellectual and volitional control we must first possess it.*

He restates this point elsewhere (1966: 44) giving it a slightly different connotation:

(3) *We might formulate the general genetic law of cultural development as follows: any function in the child's cultural development appears on the stage twice, on two planes, first on the social plane and then on the psychological, first among people as an intermental category and then within the child as an intramental category.*

Putting these three points together, it can be said that since meaning is objectively inherent in the child's social interactions with his mother (the intermental level), the child is performing in accord with Vygotsky's criterion, he already possesses a function, that of producing meaningful actions. Since he possesses it he may later be able to subject it to intellectual and volitional control (the intramental level), by receiving "instruction" from an adult. Through the mother's responses to the child's action they are constituted in Mead's terms as gestures.

What the child has to accomplish is the ability to use these socially constituted gestures deliberately. He does not have to learn how to produce meaningful behaviour, only how to control the production of that behaviour. He learns this control by having his actions reflected for him by someone else. Shotter (1974b) maintains that:

A child monitors his actions for their meaning not their *forms*. It is attending to the form of a performance while at the same time monitoring it for its meaning that even the most highly practised performers find difficult. Treating another person's *actions* as a *sequence of events* is a service one person can provide to another, a service that is essential if one's performance is to be structured into juxtaposed parts which can then be arranged and rearranged as one pleases—skilful behaviour.

This "treating another person's actions as a sequence of events" can be thought of as a form of "instruction": so likewise can treating those actions *as if* they were meaningful. "Instruction" can then be appreciated not as some formal activity, but as something that is continually occurring all around us. For example, your laughter can inform me of the meaning of my actions, or of the fact that I have performed them in the wrong sequence: your laughing is a form of instruction.

In this way the social process is responsible for the creation of new objects. For example, the concept of "eating" is a social object when viewed as an *act*. No two events that may be termed "eating" are likely to be composed of identical actions. Many different performances may constitute the act of eating, but all these performances have to satisfy certain criteria to be identified as an instance of the act. The existence of these new objects provides the socialized person with objective criteria by which to judge or treat "another person's actions as a meaningful sequence of events". It is by reference to these objective criteria that the child's actions are reflected back to him by his mother, a representative of the culture he has been born into: for in reflecting his actions back to him the mother gives him the opportunity of making an agreement with her over the value of those actions. Through the process of agreement the child is endowed with his culture's criteria for making perceptual judgements.

The external reflection of the child's actions is only implicated in the constitution of the *social* objects or events; these things he comes to have common knowledge of. Biological and certain physical attributes of "things as objects or events" can be constituted by the child's own reflection upon his non-social actions to yield *individual* objects (cf. the orthodox Piagetian concept of "reflective intelligence" and its implication in the sensori-motor stage of cognitive development). The essence of these distinctions is that knowledge can only be gained from an interaction with some entity if criteria are available for judging that entity and creating a value for it. And the child is in possession of criteria for constituting entities as both physical objects—he can acquire knowledge of hardness and softness, for example—and as biological objects—he can, for example, acquire knowledge of food and drink by himself. He possesses these criteria from birth. Since no other being is involved in the creation of this knowledge, the objects which the child knows in these ways can be termed individual objects. In the case of social objects, by contrast, the child is not in possession of criteria with which to constitute the activites he sees as exemplars of certain acts—only his mother knows these. Consequently it is necessary to think of reflection not only in the Piagetian sense, where the child spontaneously reflects upon his own actions, but also in this second sense, where his social actions are reflected back to him, not by himself initially, but by his mother.

A concrete example is useful here. Suppose the child wriggles, cries, waves his arms, and so on. His mother will take only the cry as a gesture—treating it as a form of demand or request. She possesses cultural criteria which enable her to treat this portion of his activities as having this function. But the child cannot do the same. He performs many actions, one of which is crying, and in so doing gains a response from his mother. However, he has no way of knowing which of these actions his mother is acting upon. It is only through his continued immersion in social activities, through the continual treatment of his actions as a *sequence of events* that he comes to objectify crying, to use it as the effective action, and to perceive its meaning.

3.2 Gesture and language

The three points made in the previous section lead to the theoretical expectation that the child will develop a gestural communicative ability as a result of his transactions with his mother. Further, a potential relation may be anticipated between this gestural ability and the child's later emerging linguistic one. This suggestion is by no means a new one, for there exists a traditional idea in studies of child language that gestures may have a deal of relevance to language development. For example, McCarthy (1954: 521) notes that:

> It is quite generally agreed that the child understands gestures before he understands words and, in fact, that he uses gestures himself long before he uses language proper . . . . It has been claimed that words constitute substitutes for actual gross motor activity.

One such claim has been made by Latif (1934: 76). He states that:

> It is through the intervention of its elders that the general movements and postures of an infant gradually pass into symbolic gestures.

There exist, however, two powerful objections against such claims, both closely related.

The first is that Latif's "general movements and postures" have different meanings for the different individuals involved, the elders and the infant—"the conversation of gestures does not carry with it a symbol which has a universal significance to all the different individuals" (Mead, 1934: 55). Thus, while through the effects of their reflection in social interactions, the infant's movements and postures may attain to a vestigial state, they cannot become directly symbolic. The second objection relates to McCarthy's views (1954) concerning gestures and their possible relation to language, i.e. that words are substituted for gestures in a pre-established gestural system, and has a similar basis. Bruner (1976) notes that this type of view—he deals with de Laguna's (1927) formulation of gestural importance, and not specifically that of McCarthy—is certainly helpful, because it allows us to see a developmental continuity that makes the appearance of words a less problematic occurrence. But it does not remove all the problems in his view, as it cannot provide an account "for the development of truth functions, and certainly not for the mastery of the linguistic form that predication takes in surface structures". It is on the latter points that I now want to take issue with Bruner through a return to Mead's work.

Thus far Mead's concept of the gesture has been introduced in a very general way. He goes on to offer a more rigorous definition: a gesture is "that phase of the individual act to which adjustment takes place on the part of other individuals in the social process of behaviour" (1934: 46). They are "movements of the first organism which act as specific stimuli calling forth the (socially) appropriate responses of the second organism" (1934: 14). With respect to the fact that gestures can constitute an objective field of meaning without the participating organisms being aware of that meaning themselves, Mead subdivides gesture into two categories, unconscious (non-significant) or conscious (significant) gestures:

> The conversation of gestures is not significant below the human level, because it is not conscious, that is, not self-conscious (though it is conscious in the sense of involving feelings or sensations). An animal as opposed to a human form, in indicating something to, or bringing out a meaning for, another form, is not at the same time indicating or bringing out the same thing or meaning to or for himself . . . . A gesture is not significant when the response of another organism to it does not indicate to the organism making it what the other organism is responding to.
>
> (Mead, 1934: 81)

It is from these grounds that Mead develops his view of language and the language symbol:

meaning can be described, accounted for, or stated in terms of symbols or language at its highest and most complex stage of development (the stage it reaches in human experience), but language simply lifts out of the social process a situation which is logically or implicitly there already. The language symbol is simply a significant or conscious gesture.

(Mead, 1934: 79)

But I want to suggest that this is not totally correct, that language may exist at levels other than the "highest", and that developmentally it actually does so. Consequently, it becomes possible to separate the problems of the transition from gesture to language, and from the non-significant to the significant gesture. I can best clarify this with an example.

It will be argued later that crying develops such that the infant eventually uses it deliberately for the purposes of attracting his mother's attention, and for making a demand. Elsewhere (Lock, 1978), I have discussed the development of an arm-raising gesture, the child coming to use this as a demand to be lifted. Sometimes he will cry, and then raise his arms, thus intensifying and clarifying the demand. At this level his gestures are non-significant. Consider now the two-word utterance *mommy down* reported by Greenfield and Smith (1976: 93) as being used by a child aged 16 months. Here *mommy* does not refer to the mother, but appears to have developed from the total stylization of crying into a nasal phrase. It retains the same function as crying, that of attracting attention and making a demand. *Down* specifies the child's intention—to be lifted down from a chair—and thus functions to the same end as arm-raising did earlier. The two-word utterance *mommy down* has thus both the same form and use as the two-gesture com-municative act of crying and arm-raising, and developmentally the two abilities appear very closely related (for a fuller discussion see Chapter 10). Thus, in this instance McCarthy's view (1954) that "words consti-tute substitutes for actual gross motor activity" is quite correct. And therefore we have language which is really no different from the earlier non-significant gestural ability—words are being used here as "vocal gestures" rather than "language symbols".

As a result, then, we must note, firstly, that Mead's view regarding the nature of the language symbol must be modified, viz:

(4) *Language symbols may be "simply significant or conscious gestures" at their highest level—i.e. in propositional discourse—but in their early stages they may in fact be non-significant gestures.*

Secondly, that the development of truth functions in language is likely to be involved in the transition that has yet to be discussed, from the non-significant to the significant gesture. And thirdly, that there is a possible basis for "surface structure" in the general precursors of language. For example, *mommy down* is a two-word utterance and is thus open to grammatical analysis. Yet it does not follow that to account for this structure one must go beyond anything not involved in the child's gestural capabilities, such as positing him with innate linguistic abilities. For, after all, he was similarly able to combine his earlier gestures for the same end, and there is little exclusively linguistic about the form his request now takes. The question is thus raised as to what is responsible for the structural form that such an utterance shows.

3.3 Structural aspects of meaning

I want to turn yet again to Mead to take two points from his writings that are important in relation to this question of structure. The first point was given earlier; it is that

(5) *Meaning can be described, accounted for, or stated in terms of symbols or language at its highest and most complex stage of development . . . but language simply lifts out of the social process a situation which is logically or implicitly there already.*   (Mead, 1934: 79)

The second is this:

(6) *When there is (a) relation between form and environment, then objects can appear which would not have been there otherwise; but the animal does not create ( ) food in the sense that he makes an object out of nothing. Rather, when the form is put into such a relation with the environment, then there emerges such a thing as food. Wheat becomes food: just as water arises in the relation of hydrogen and oxygen.*
                                    (Mead, 1934: 333)

Here Mead is implying in a general way that it is both the social process and the child's situation in it that yields structure: that the roots of structure are to be found not *in* the child, nor *in* the environment, but in the relation between the two, with the social process mediating its emergence.

This general implication can be developed by taking the five developmental stages put forward in the last chapter one at a time. The first of these was where the child begins to use his actions in the pursuit of goals he has formulated. These goals stem in the main from his coming to apprehend the pre-established relationships necessarily existing between himself and his environment (Mead, quotation (6) above). By his very structured existence he *creates* "objects with value", and as he *discovers* those values his actions are endowed with an intentional nature. The values which structure his actions are thus themselves structured: form, relationship, environment.

However, the child's intentional actions occur within a social context, and they thus constitute social acts. It is through this constitution that the child is able to discover those pre-established relationships which structure his actions, for in interaction with him his mother reflects these actions back to him; she perceives the pre-established relationships where he does not. Thus meaning arises and is structured—for example, the mother acting towards the *child's cry* in *relation* to the *context* in which it occurs—from, relationship, environment.

Through this process of interaction the child passes to the next developmental stage: he begins to pursue his intentions through the effects of his actions—now become gestures—in the social environment. His actions have a social meaning which is perceived similarly by both the child and his mother. This agreed social meaning *implicit* in his actions is again structured: form, relationship, environment. For example, his crying communicates a relationship, positive or negative, between himself (form) and some object (environment) such as food or the nappy fastener which is sticking in (relationship) him (form), and so on. Thus the meaning implicit in the child's early social interactions is structured: and so likewise are the gestures used to communicate these implicit meanings.

In sum, two points have been made; firstly *structured* meaning is implicit in the early actions—it exists at Vygotsky's intermental level. Secondly, these early actions become intentional, and because they are generally made effective through another's agency they become elevated to the status of intentionally communicative gestures. To continue; each of these gestures can be said to explicate a certain portion of the implicit meaning of the social transactions constituted by its antecedent action. For example, pregestural crying carries the implicit structured meaning; form (I) relationship (WANT) environment (SOMETHING). Of these, crying is only perceived as making determinate the *relationship* portion; form and environment are made determinate by factors beyond the cry (see Chapters 4 and 5). But there is no reason to believe that the child at this stage intends crying to have this value, structure or eventual effect. Later there is, and then it can be said that the gesture has "lifted out of the social process a situation which is logically or implicitly there already". It is used in a definite way to make explicit a portion of an already structured meaning; to make a relationship determinate in acts of deliberate communication. This function now exists at the intramental level. Similarly when pointing develops, it makes explicit the environmental portion of the meaning its use implies. The child points at something, making it determinate to another, but leaves the other components—form and relationship—to be determined by factors beyond the action (again, see Chapter 4).

In the next stage of development, the child employs his gestures together, rather than one at a time. For example, he cries and points, making determinate both *that* he wants and *what* he wants (see Chapter 5). Finally, the form of crying changes in development, and often eventually yields the "word" *mama* (see Chapter 8); *mama* is used to make demands, and not to refer to the mother. A vocal gesture— usually classified as an early word, and hence part of language proper—thus arises directly from an earlier action ("words constitute substitutes for actual gross motor activity"). Similarly, many early words are used in conjunction with gestures such as pointing, and often in fact substitute for a gesture in the performance of the same communicative function (again see Chapter 8). Thus returning to the example *mommy down—mommy* and words substituted for gestures merely give explicit form to the meanings implied by their historical antecedents.

In summary, then, gestures arise in the interactions between people, in the communicative acts they share. At the height of their development these gestures show all the rudiments of language and at least in some cases, patterned speech results from the internalization of the structure of these shared acts (as, in similar vein, Piaget argues that thought arises from the internalization of action). Likewise, meanings initially exist between the interactants—Vygotsky's "intermental level"—and only later with the development of symbols are they internalized and simultaneously given explicit form—Vygotsky's "intramental level". Mead (1934: 79) maintains similarly that meaning is objectively present in any social conduct between individuals, and that "language simply lifts out of the social process a situation which is logically or implicitly there already". It is implicitly there, *both functionally and structurally,* and given explicit form, first through the gesture and then through the vocal gesture. The next problem to examine is that of the development of the *language symbol* itself.

3.4 The transition from vocal gesture to language symbol: the development of propositional speech

The development of the language symbol can be elucidated after a discussion of two concepts: those of *emergence* and *proposition*.

3.4.1 Emergence

It is Popper (1972) in his theory of "World 3", who best characterizes emergent phenomena. In discussing evolution in almost its entire range he makes use of notions of three different "worlds": the objective world of material things, which he terms World 1, the subjective world of minds, World 2; and World 3, comprised of objective structures which are the products of minds or living things—language, law, science, art, institutions—in a word, culture. Magee (1973: 59–60) provides a useful exposition of Popper's views:

> the individual (primitive man) came into a world dominated by abstractions—kinship relation, forms of social organisation and government, law, custom, convention, tradition, alliances and enmities, ritual, religion, superstition, language—all of which were man-made but none of them made by *him,* or even open to questioning by him. As against each man, then, they stood as a kind of objective reality, shaping him from birth, making him human, determining almost everything about his life, yet quasi-autonomous. It is Popper's contention that most such things were never planned or intended. "How does an animal path in the jungle arise? Some animal may break through the undergrowth in order to get to a drinking-place. Other animals find it easiest to use the same track. Thus it may be widened and improved by use. It is not planned—it is an unintended consequence of the need for easy or swift movement. This is how a path is originally made—perhaps even by men—and how language and any other institutions which are useful may arise, and how they may owe their existence and development to their usefulness. They are not planned or intended, and there was perhaps no need for them before they came into existence. But they may create a new need, or a new set of aims: the aim-structure of animals or men is not "given" but it develops, with the help of some kind of feedback mechanism, out of earlier aims, and out of the results which were or were not aimed at. In this way, a whole new universe of possibilities or potentialities may arise: a world which is to a large extent autonomous. (Popper, 1972: 119–8)."

As an example of this autonomy Popper discusses the properties of mathematics. He maintains that the sequence of natural numbers is a human construction;

> But although we create this sequence, it creates its own autonomous problems in its turn. The distinction between odd and even numbers is not created by us: it is an unintended and unavoidable consequence of our creation. Prime numbers, of course, are similarly unintended and objective facts; and in their case it is obvious that there are many facts here for us to *discover*: there are conjectures like Goldbach's [that every even number is the sum of two primes: this fits every known case, but a proof of it has yet to be provided, A. L.]. And these conjectures, though they refer indirectly to objects of our creation refer directly to problems and facts which have somehow emerged from our creation and which we cannot control or influence: they are hard facts, and the truth about them is often hard to discover. This exemplifies what I mean when I say that the third world is largely autonomous, though created by us.
>
> (Popper, 1972: 118)

Popper's ideas are of relevance here in two ways. Firstly his mathematical example can serve as a direct analogy to the child who is developing language. Assume that the first "language forms" a child uses are in fact numbers; one, two, three, four and so on. These numbers are a human construction, more importantly they are a construction of the child—"the language is 'reinvented' each time it is learned" (Chomsky, 1968: 75)—but they bring with them properties which only emerge upon their having been created, those "unintended and purely unavoidable" properties such as odd and even, perfect and prime numbers. Assume further that these unintended consequences are ones upon which the adult language is based: that in order to progress to the adult form of speech the infant has to realize these properties for his own use. That is to say, in order to further his development he has to discover these new objects which are implicit in what he has already created. Thus, by learning the first few numbers the child opens up "a whole new universe of possibilities and potentialities" which he must make actual in order to develop: to develop into the adult form of language is to make actual in behaviour these emergent properties of a previous creation, to give explicit form to their implications. To look at development through this analogy is to conceive of the child as a problem-solver, solving problems he sets himself with each new ability he develops; and in successfully solving each of these problems he progresses on the path to possessing the adult language.

Further, Popper's ideas lead to a second point that is developed in later chapters (Chapters 10 and 11): that grammar in the child's language may be an artifact which has nothing whatsoever to do with the way in which he learns that language. To put this back in Popper's terms for a moment to clarify the point: if one considers a child learning mathematics, or even learning to count, one does not assume that because what he has learnt exhibits certain principles, such as odd and even numbers, his learning has been in any way guided by these principles. The fact that what he has learnt exhibits such things is purely coincidential and merely the result of his learning. Similarly then with the child's emerging language, the fact that it possesses a grammatical structure in no way necessitates positing in him innate grammatical knowledge to account for this structure's existence: grammar may be an automomous creation of language use that we, as scientists, have great difficulty in discovering, but which the child has no difficulty in producing, since it is a totally unintended aspect of what he is doing and has somehow emerged from it. Thus by concentrating on a search for autonomous, innate grammars we, as scientists, may be barking up entirely the wrong tree.

It is this conception of developmental processes that underlies the arguments presented later. The major contention is that through interaction with his mother the child is engaged in a process of developing communicative behaviours, which contain by their very nature such implicit emergent phenomena. By establishing meaningful communication between themselves, the mother and child open up a "whole new universe of possibilities and potentialities" some of which comprise the "problems" the child has to surmount in progressing towards a fully fledged language. The mother is as much involved in the surmounting of them as is the child, and thus it becomes necessary to rewrite Chomsky's point (1968: 75) in the following way: *language emerges through a process of guided reinvention.* The mother is the guide and the child the inventor.

3.4.2 Propositions

The concept of a proposition is closely linked with that of predication. Current fashion amongst logicians sees propositions as bearers of truth and falsity—and obviously they are bearers of such truths about something or other. In other words, a proposition is a statement that relates one object to another in a way that is open to being judged true or false. The linguistic form of such a statement will involve some variety of predication by definition. Consequently, a proposition can be defined as having the following properties: (i) *it relates one object to another;* and (ii) that relationship can be judged for its *truth or falsity, and could be found to be false.*

By this definition, the implied meanings of certain non-verbal communicative acts can be judged as to whether or not they are propositional in structure. In general such "statements" made about the state of the world, of some object in it, or of the actor at some time other than that at which the "statement" is made, are propositional by the above definition. However, a separate category of similar "statements" does not necessarily imply propositional meanings: "statements" concerning firstly, the present state, desires or wishes of the actor, and secondly the "naming" of objects.

To expand on this, *some* statements concerning the actor's present state, etc. certainly are propositional. An example would be the groans made by a malingerer. To be a malingerer one must be able to treat oneself as an object and be able to lie. But if an adult who is *actually* ill utters similar groans, they are no longer of a propositional nature: their implied meaning refers to subjectively experienced states which *actually* exist for the actor. His groans could not thus be judged as true or false "statements" and be found to be false. Splitting hairs further, the child who cries, even if deliberately, because he is hungry, is again not functioning at a propositional level of implied meaning. Firstly, if the cry is linked to the subjective state of hunger and the child cries, then he is hungry, full stop; and secondly, the pre-language-symbol child is unable to treat himself as an object in the world—he does not possess self-awareness. His statement thus could not be found to be false, and nor does it relate one object to another. Therefore, it is not "propositional".

Similarly, utterances used in a primitive referential way are not propositional as again they do not relate one object to another: they only assert, in the case of naming, the identity of an object. For us as adults, we could say that naming is propositional since it relates the objectively existent name of the object to the given object itself. But for the child who does not possess words as objects, he is essentially relating one object to itself (see Chapter 9 for a further discussion on this topic). Thus while he may use the wrong name with respect to an object, consequently allowing his utterance to be judged as false, his utterance is not propositional since it does not relate one object to another.

Yet if the gestures the child uses in his intended acts of communication, and his early words used "referentially" towards objects are not *actually* propositional, they are at least *potentially* so. Ignoring at present "object-naming" utterances, the following may be said with respect to gestural communication. Firstly, a specific communicative act may imply the meaning *I want food* (Sanborn suggests allowing structured, non-linguistic but meaningful communications to be validly given a "translation" into the adult mode of expression—see also Section 1.3 and Chapter 5). In that act, the relationship and environment components of the message can be made explicit by the child's actions of crying and pointing (see Chapter 6 for a discussion of the use of gestures in combination). The form component (I) remains implicit, the child not being able to refer to himself at the time in question. But this act will effectively become propositional when the child can perceive himself as an object and make explicit the implied form (I). Secondly, such a communicative act—having the meaning (I) WANT FOOD—implies further implicit meanings which are of a propositional nature—(YOU) (GIVE) (ME) (FOOD). According to Mead, language must somehow make these potential and implied propositions explicit—it must lift them out of social interaction. The problem, then, is how this lifting out occurs.

3.4.3 The explication of the implied proposition form: the language symbol

Chapter 9 argues that the vocal gesture in both its "referential" (object-labelling: implying the meaning structured THAT IS *WORD*) and communicative (intention-pursuing: implying the meaning I WANT *WORD*) uses opens up the possibility of explicit propositional use (an *emergent* possibility) *and* provides the "tools" by which that possibility is made actual. The argument is that once the child is in possession of, firstly, the ability to use a communicative act with the values WANT and OBJECT made explicit, and secondly possesses the "referential" word-function of object-labelling, he possesses the tools for explicating *all* the components of the implied meanings (e.g. *you give me that*) of his acts with the value *I want that*. Having accomplished this explication, the vocal gestures that provide the tools whereby the process occurs become self-transformed to the status of language symbols. The "mechanics" of this transformation are given a full discussion in Chapter 9, so need not be pursued here. Chapter 11 notes that the ultimate explication is of the implicit object *I*, resulting in self-awareness, and comments on the apparently roundabout manner of its appearance.

The approach to the problem of language development put forward here, then, is that the majority of the child's early words may be considered as *vocal gestures* having two historic roots: firstly, a communicative function, the development of which can be traced back right to the earliest transactions the child has with the real world; and secondly, a referential function, which likewise has preverbal antecedents, although these are not given an extensive treatment hereafter. These two functions in combination open up the possibility of propositional speech—i.e. the appearance of the *language symbol*—and provide the means whereby this possibility is actualized. Chapters 4 and 6 deal with the first two developments. Chapter 9 discusses the process whereby the vocal gesture is transformed into the language symbol.

Allied to the above, the approach to human development that emerges here revolves around the fact that meaning is objectively inherent in the child's social interaction with his mother. The mother is able to monitor consciously both her own and her child's behaviour for these meanings. She makes these meanings determinate to herself in accordance with objectified criteria embodied in both her language and the way she perceives the world. She is thus able to treat large portions of his behaviour as meaningful, *and thus as having an objective form.* Through acting towards her child on the basis of her perceptions of him she brings out for him these objective values of his actions through making them effective—she reflects his behaviour back to him—and thus she functions to create those actions as objects for the child himself. She is further instrumental in this way in constituting the "mental operations" by which her child eventually deals with the "objective reality" she has helped him create. The process of *guided reinvention* can thus be seen to be of crucial importance: the paths to language, self-awareness, and eventual existence as a "socialized" adult are all traversed by the individual through the process of guided reinvention.

3.5 Need-determination

Bloom (1973) maintains that language emerges as a linguistic coding of prior cognitive abilities, abilities which are concerned with the *relationships* between objects in the child's environment. In other words her view, along with that of many contemporary writers, is that language codes knowledge. Thus any enquiry into language development must be concerned with the growth of the child's knowledge; and one is then faced with the problem of what does it grow from, what are the origins of this knowledge, what might its nature be. In what follows I will assume that at birth the child possesses innate criteria by which to make sense of his experiences in the world, and thus may "create" his own knowledge in the course of encountering the world.

What might these criteria be? One suggestion might be that they are constituted by our experiences of our bodily needs: that at birth the human organism has neither mind nor knowledge, but rather possesses inbuilt bodily criteria by which to judge the relationship between impinging sense data from the world he has been born into and the results of his natural, spontaneous actions in that world. The child himself would thus be capable of relating events in the world to his actions, and thereby able to begin to act with expectations of what can be accomplished, to create and possess knowledge.

The origins of this viewpoint are to be found in Dreyfus' (1967) critique of the two basic assumptions of workers in the field of artificial intelligence. These assumptions are:

(1) An epistemological assumption that all intelligent behaviour can be simulated by a device whose only mode of information processing is that of a detached, disembodied, objective observer.
(2) The ontological assumption, related to logical atomism, that everything essential to intelligent behaviour can in principle be understood in terms of a determinate set of independent elements. In brief . . . the belief that all that is essential to human intelligence can be formalised.

(Dreyfus, 1967: 14)

Dreyfus suggests that this paradigm of research, however intrinsically implausible, "gains persuasiveness from the absence of an alternative account" and he attempts to provide one. It is from his alternative account of a form of non-detached, non-disembodied, non-objective, structure-dependent, practical knowledge that the view presented below is derived.

Dreyfus notes that, firstly, no one has yet suggested how a machine could structure the information given to it as *relevent* or *irrelevant* to the problem to be solved, nor how this ability could be learned. Furthermore, "in creative problem solving we do not know what our goal is until we have achieved it. We do not have a list of determinate objective specifications which the solution must fulfil" (p. 25). How, then, as humans, are we able to structure our experiences as significant or insignificant? Dreyfus answers this by an appeal to "concrete bodily needs":

> When we experience a need we do not at first know what it is we need. We must search to discover what allays our restlessness or discomfort. This is not found by comparing various objects and activities with some objective, determinate criterion, but through . . . our sense of gratification. This gratification is experienced as the discovery of what we needed all along, but it is a retroactive understanding and covers up the fact that we were unable to make our need determinate without first receiving that gratification. The original fulfilment of any need is, therefore . . . a creative discovery. Only such an analysis of human needs can both account for our ability to order our experience in terms of relevance and significance and at the same time allow determination of the goal of creative problem solving to remain part of the problem-solving task.
>
> (1967: 25–26)

Further, Dreyfus provides an account of how one could perform physical tasks without in any way appealing to formal principles as follows:

> Consider the act of randomly waving my hand in the air. I am not trying to place my objective hand at an objective point in space. To perform this waving I need not take into account the geometry, since I am not attempting any specific achievement. Now suppose that, in this random thrashing about, I happen to touch something, and that this satisfies and thereby makes partially determinate a need, a need to cope with things. I can then repeat *whatever I did*—this time *in order to* touch something—without appealing to the laws necessary to describe it as a physical motion. I now have a way of bringing two objects together in objective space without appealing to any principle except: "Do that again". This is the way skills are built up. The important thing about skills is that, although *science* requires that the skilled performance be *described* according to rules, these rules need in no way be *involved* in producing the performance. (1967: 29).

The relevance of Dreyfus' account here is that it describes how the child's inherent "concrete bodily needs" can function as criteria by which the world may be judged. During the early period of his life the child may gain an organized perspective upon his activity; using his specific bodily needs as criteria he may make his actions both take on values and become determinate. He moves from "random thrashing about" to "Do that again"; he creatively discovers, delineates and makes determinate purposes for his actions. Through a combination of acting in the world and possessing bodily needs as the criteria by which to judge his actions, the child may build up a body of practical knowledge relevant to his own needs.

But the infant does not live solely a biological existence, he also lives in both social and cultural worlds, or in MacMurray's terms "he lives a common life as one term in a personal relation" (1961: 50). Thus not only are the criteria by which the child initially judges the world important, but so also are those a mother uses to judge both the child and the world in which they live together. The successful actions which result in the child making his "retroactive creative discoveries", and thereby making his bodily states determinate, are in most cases selected and segmented by the mother. Richards (1974a: 88) points out that

> it is . . . often assumed that in our own culture crying is the major signal that the infant uses to indicate his hunger to his mother and so regulate the pattern of feeds . . . even if this can be shown to be true in Europe and America, it is not universal. Among the !Kung bushmen where infants are carried on the mother's body, the infant's movements seem to be the usual indication to the mother that the infant requires access to the breast. Crying is used to signal emergencies (Konner, 1972).

While the child is biologically capable of determining the values of his actions, which value goes with which action is determined socially and culturally through the mother's agency.

3.6 Knowledge related to needs

Turning now to the nature of the child's knowledge, there is no need to credit the child at this stage with any functional knowledge beyond a bodily-structured form: i.e. his knowledge does not have any objective basis. Knowledge of this form may be conceived as in Fig. 3.1, the child recognizing or knowing his need-states in terms of the actions he

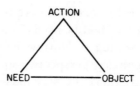

Fig. 3.1. Bodily structured knowledge.

performs in reducing them and the "substrate" he performs those
actions upon; his actions in terms of their value in gratifying a need: and
the gratifying "object" in terms of the valued action *vis-à-vis* the need
state. In constrast, objective knowledge of one's actions may be given as
in Fig. 3.2. Parenthetically, it may be noted that while the child's

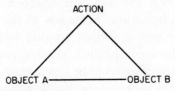

Fig. 3.2. Objectively structured knowledge.

knowledge has no *actual* objective basis, it has the potential for attaining
to such a form. The child is gaining a knowledge of "things" in the
outside world as objects in relation to his need-states and the actions he
can perform upon these things. In this way he begins to recognize and
classify objects, and it is implicit in such a classification that objects are
being related to each other—potential objective knowledge exists:

> an ever-growing number of objects come to be included in the schema's
> field of application, come to be subsumed within the sensory-motor
> category of "something to suck", ... the infant gradually comes to
> "recognise", in the most primitive possible sense of the term, that some
> objects are "suckable and nourishing" (breast, bottle, etc.) and others
> "suckable and non-nourishing" (fingers, blanket, etc.)—thus, for instance,
> the infant becomes more abrupt and definite in his rejection of the latter
> when hungry.   (Flavell, 1963: 90)

A potential bridge thus exists between these two forms of knowledge
which the child later unintentionally crosses (see Chapters 9, 10 and
11).

Similarly a bridge exists between these early intentional activities
and the child's later communicative abilities. The developing child's
behaviour has two aspects: there are those behaviours related to the
establishment of an ability, and those that *exploit* an ability. For example,
the child slowly establishes the values of his actions, and is then later
able to exploit these actions "at will". In Vygotsky's terms he must
develop an ability through spontaneous action before he can employ
that ability deliberately. For example, in making use of "Do that
again" behaviours the child does not initially take any account of the

locus of responsibility for "doing that again". His initial assumption appears to be that in all cases it is his own action, and thus his own agency, that is responsible for the event in question. At this stage he is incapable of distinguishing between those actions which effect changes in the world directly, and those that only do so through their effect on another agent. Through future actions and their outcomes this distinction will become explicit. He will thus establish a mode of acting in which he can put his behaviour not solely to the end of relieving his need-state, but to the end of getting another to perform the actions necessary for this to be accomplished. He thus establishes the level of communication by exploiting what he can already do. This level happens to be a new one for the child, in that he has now become able not only to control his own behaviour in the pursuit of specific ends, but that of others as well (for example, Peter in Observations 5–11).

Establishment and exploitation bear a relationship akin to the Piagetian dichotomy of assimilation and accommodation, in that they are inseparable in reality. The course of the child's development is determined by the outcome of those actions he performs—and by implication, and most importantly, those he does *not* perform. The child cannot establish any new scheme of action without first exploiting those actions he possesses: in establishing one level he exploits the possibilities of previous levels, and in exploiting one level he establishes new ones. Exploitation can establish new levels, by opening up new possibilities to the child which transcend his earlier behaviour, but this only occurs through the child making new distinctions in his ambiguous behaviours. He must come to realize the nature of what he is responsible for to realize the implications of his actions. This concept of implications and the way they may be drawn out by the child from his own behaviour is discussed in more detail in Chapter 9.

The way in which the mother is able to perceive the child's actions as meaningful has already been noted above. More rigorously it may be stated that her judgements serve to delineate the act-structures within which she and the child will operate. Since the behaviours of the neonate are undifferentiated in terms of value to him, he does not possess any categories for his behaviour—his actions are not "modularized" (cf. Bruner, 1974)—and as such they have no objective existence, no beginning, middle or end. However, the mother is able to perform this categorization, and by introducing value into the child's actions she effectively begins to structure them for him, creating beginnings and ends to what he does. In this way the mother and her child function together as a dyad to negotiate values for each others actions, the value of any action being dependent upon the context of the acts which it comes to constitute (see below for an example). Thus the child begins to segment his activities within the categories of the acts to which they are subordinated.

To return to the simplified situation of the child experiencing discomfort and consequently crying in a reflex manner: it is because the internal states of the child have external consequences that the mother is alerted to the child's condition. She treats the cry as a message informing her that all is not well. What it is that is "not well" is delineated by contextual information. Thus it is possible to give to this interactive behaviour a structural description in terms of the mother perceiving the child's cry as a communicative act, in which the cry serves to inform the mother that the child is in a state of need, and the context within which the cry occurs enables her to delineate what that need might be. The cry is given its value by the context within which it is perceived by the mother, and she reflects this value back to the child in her subsequent actions.

Further, it may be expected that as he grows older, he will be able to recognize, to a greater and greater extent, the state he is in, and have some knowledge of how that state may be removed. Qualitative changes occurring in the child's behaviour provide evidence to back up these expectations. Firstly, the child's rooting behaviour becomes less global in its application; and secondly, it comes to be used in anticipation. For example, to repeat Piaget's (1951) observation again, he notes that at the end of the second month "Laurent only tries to nurse when he is in his mother's arms and no longer when on the dressing table" (p. 58). Again he observes,

Lucienne at 0;3(12) stops crying when she sees her mother unfastening her dress for the meal.

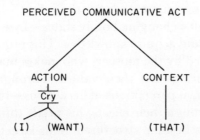

Fig. 3.3. Structural description of mother's perception of child's cry.

Laurent, too, between 0;3(15) and 0;4 reacts to visual signals. When, after being dressed as usual just before the meal, he is put in my arms in position for nursing, he looks at me and then searches all around, looks at me again, etc.—but he does not attempt to nurse. When I place him in his mother's arms without his touching the breast, he looks at her and immediately opens his mouth wide, cries, moves about, in short reacts in a completely significant way. It is therefore sight and no longer the position which henceforth is the signal.   (Piaget, 1951: 60)

Similarly Ripin (1930), studying sucking responses in anticipation of feeding during the first six months of life, found occasional anticipatory responses as early as the first month, but concluded after examining all her data that true expectancies were not established until the third months of life.

Popper sees the growth of knowledge as being the result of problem-solving (1972: 242). Vygotsky's (1962) position that before any activity can be subjected to voluntary control it must first exist spontaneously has already been noted. These two views give a coherent perspective on these present developmental changes: the child is faced with the problem of discovering the effects or values of his spontaneous actions, and once he has done this he possesses the tools whereby he can employ these actions deliberately. The child is spontaneously capable of communicating with his mother without any knowledge. She treats his actions as "gestures" and accords them values which relate both to his biological states and his social world. Consequently, he becomes able to act with knowledge, and thus also to use his gestures with knowledge. The problem faced by the infant is to discover how he accomplishes what he does "unawares": to use the knowledge he gains through this discovery to control his actions in order to accomplish what are now goals. Dreyfus' (1967) "need-determination" paradigm allows this process to be adequately characterized.

To summarize the arguments here: the infant is being viewed as possessing criteria—his changing bodily states—by which to judge his actions in the world and acquire knowledge. This process of knowledge development is guided by the mother, who makes many of his actions effective and thus brings out their values. Through doing this she changes the child's own perceptions of his actions—the child comes to know his actions through their effects, his needs through his actions, etc.—his perceptions become structured. This structuring affects the way the child is able to employ his actions: at a simple level he can anticipate. Secondly, these actions function, by virtue of the child's living in a social world, as non-significant gestures (cf. Mead, 1934) even though they are produced without any voluntary or intentional control, and initially also without knowledge. As knowledge develops so does the child's control of his actions, and he begins to direct them to the pursuit of specific goals. Initially the mother perceives the child's actions as having such-and-such meaning: in making this perception she formulates a goal for the child's actions. Further, her acting out of her perceptions creates values for the child's actions, such that he comes to formulate his own goals and direct his actions towards them. This is the essence and importance of early communication.

4. The development of gestures and goals

4.1 The establishment of gestures

The emerging knowledge of the child is built up, then, as a result of relationships constructed through his own actions. For the child the actions which the mother interprets as indicating his bodily state are in fact part of an active attempt to attain some end. If the child identifies his bodily state, he does so in terms of the actions required in reducing it: he does not simply recognize a state as "hunger", but as a state that can be removed by certain actions being performed upon certain objects. This means that from the psychological point of view it is impossible to ascribe an interpretation such as "I am hungry" to the child's early activities: the child does not know of his states in this detached, passive, contemplative way.

The distinction between detached and more "involved" forms of knowledge is not often made. For instance in a paper discussing the nature of early language development, Ingram (1971) ignores it. I think this leads him on occasion to a wrong interpretation of his data. In one instance he takes the observation reported by Luken's (1896: 434):

> After feelings of hunger, wetness, cold, fear, anger, sleepiness, etc., have been discriminated, crying acquires a speech significance, and the mood

of the child may be perceived by the variations in its voice, all of which helps mightily in the case of very young children.

He uses it within the scheme he puts forward for grammatical development as shown in Fig. 4.1. Such an interpretation gives the

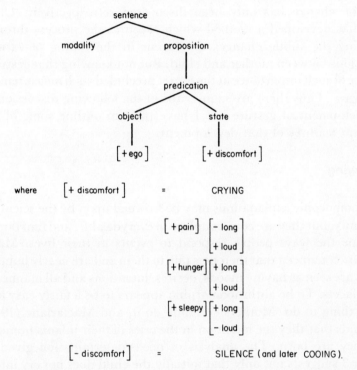

Fig. 4.1. An illustration of Ingram's (1971) scheme. (From D. Ingram (1971) Transitivity in child language. *Language* **47**: 888–910. © Linguistic Society of America. Reproduced by permission.)

impression of passivity, that the child is *stating* his needs by crying as opposed to crying in this instance being *part of an active attempt to satisfy these needs.*

Crying in early life is of a reflex nature, and as such is not at inception part of this active attempt. It *is* a reaction to a state. However, crying cannot be adequately considered in this isolated context alone, for it is through what happens *after* the child cries that his crying gradually takes on its significance. In having a value assigned to it by others, crying comes to have a social value for him and in so doing it changes its status. Through crying the child is able to determine his needs and to place values upon the objects that are implicated in the activity of determining it. On this basis he comes to be able to cry in situations in which he "knows" what he wants: his cry can come to have the value "I want that". It can be used by the child to express an intended relationship between himself and some object or event.

It is not easy to give a detailed account of how this change occurs when the change has only been discovered retrospectively. Clark (1978) has developed a method which captures the process through measuring the subtle changes that occur in the timing of various interactions between mother and child. But not knowing that gestures would be of such importance at the outset precluded such measurement in this case. Thus there are many gaps in the following discussion of the development of gesture but I have tried to outline some of the important features of that development.

4.1.1 Crying

Anthropomorphic explanations may be frowned upon by the scientific community, but they are commonplace in everyday life, and function to determine the ways people respond to events in their lives. Many people are convinced that their pets talk to them and are nearly human: animals are seen as having moods, desires, intentions and all manner of human facets. To be anthropomorphic appears to be a fairly easy and natural thing to do. Mothers certainly do it, and Macfarlane (1974, 1977) finds that they see intention in the cries of their infants immediately they are born. The analysis of needs-determination given in Chapter 3 suggests not only that initially the child does not cry intentionally, but also that he has no knowledge of what he might be crying about: he does not know *that* he wants, *what* he wants, or how he may be able to attain it. Babies are treated, however, as if they did know these things, and mothers will go so far as questioning them as to their motives:

Observation 23
Paul; age 6 (19): Paul is sitting alone in the middle of the livingroom. He starts to cry. Mother comes into the room.
Mother: Oh, now what's up, hey? Oh dear, Oh dear, what's the matter?
She picks him up.
Mother: Are you thirsty, is that what it is? Do you want a drink?
She goes and picks up his bottle and offers it to him.
He refuses it and continues crying.

Mother: Hungry? Are you? Do you want something to eat? No? Sleepy then,
   do you want to go to sleep?
She puts him in his pram but he continues to cry. She picks him up again and
walks about comforting him. She stops at the window. Paul apparently looks
out but continues crying. Mother tries to attract his attention, and then to
direct it.
Mother: Look, there's a pussycat, can you see him? Do you know what
   pussycats say? Do you? They say "miaow" don't they, yes, of course
   they do.
Paul stops crying during this speech.
Mother: There, that's better, down you go then. She places him back on the
   floor.

It is quite possible in this observation that Paul had no determinate
need behind his actions, that they constituted "random thrashing
about". None the less, the mother attempts to deal with her child: she
perceives his crying *as if* it were some sensible communication being
addressed to her by him. This example also shows quite clearly how
she goes about making sense of the message. The child's crying can only
function to alert her to some "need" in the child, the cry tells her *that* he
needs something, but not *what* that something might be. Since the child
is sitting on his own in the middle of a room there is little in his
environment that she can relate to his crying, and thus she has to go
through a long process of trying to isolate some specific reason for his
crying. Similarly in the following observation, there is little available
for the mother to use to make sense of the child's crying:

Observation 24
Mary; age 7 (27): Mary is sitting in her high chair at the table, having just
finished her feed. She cries loudly and sharply.
Mother: What's the matter? Do you want your potty?
Mary cries again, and mother notices her drinking cup in front of her is nearly
empty. Mother picks it up and says, "Do you want any more?" but she then
puts the cup down and proceeds to wash Mary's face. Mary cries again, and
mother says, "All right then", and goes out of the room to fetch the potty.

What she does is to guess, firstly from the time of the crying and in line
with her own intentions for the child—Mary is just starting potty-
training—and secondly she tries some environmental feature.
   On other occasions the context in which the child cries makes the
task of interpretation easier; for example:

Observation 25

Paul; age 10 (21): Paul is again sitting in the middle of the floor but is not alone. He is sitting next to a dog. He pokes it, leans on it, pulls its fur. The dog gets up and moves away to sit down somewhere else. Paul crawls after it and resumes poking it. The "game" continues in this way. Mother comes in from the kitchen and watches.

Mother: I don't think he wants to play, do you? Go on out and get some peace.

She lets the dog out. Paul remains quiet for a while, and then starts crying.

Mother: Oh, all right.

She opens the door and whistles. On the dog's reappearance Paul stops crying.

Here there is an immediate uncertainty as to the nature and meaning of Paul's crying: the child cannot be asked if the mother's interpretation was correct. Paul may be crying with the intention of expressing that he wants the dog brought back, in response to its having gone away, or neither. As it is, only the fact that he stopped crying when the dog came back suggests that the mother's interpretation was correct.

Parenthetically, it is interesting to note two things about this observation. Firstly the mother is able to perceive the dog as having needs which he expresses by his actions in exactly the same way as she perceives them in her child. And secondly, Paul and the dog are engaged in a process of negotiation between themselves which is very similar to that which goes on between any infant and mother. Both the above points stem from the fact that Paul's actions towards the dog take on their value from the dog's reaction to them. Thus the mother can perceive Paul as "tormenting" the dog, and Paul is negotiatively discovering that if he "wants" to play with the dog his present actions are inappropriate: he determines successful actions through interaction.

Treating these three previous observations at their simplest level, one can say that the child's actions are being perceived by the mother as acts of communication, in which crying is interpreted with the value of *want* and the context of the crying allows whatever is wanted to be apprehended. What the mother is doing is creating, through her interpretation, a value for the child's action: and by her subsequent behaviour allowing the child some insight into what that value is.

At this point Vygotsky's views on mental development become very important. These views were firstly, that "in order to subject a function to intellectual and volitional control, we must first possess it" (1962: 90); and secondly, "any function in the child's cultural development appears on the stage twice, on two planes, first on the social plane and then on the psychological, first among people as an intermental category and then within the child an an intramental category" (1966: 44). These two points place the mother's constructive perception of her child's behaviour in the following light: firstly, the child possesses in his activities a communicative function, and further this function exists solely on the social plane, as an intermental category. Secondly, the mother's actions toward the child on the basis of her perceptions of him will create knowledge for the child about the value of his activities. And finally he may be expected to gain a voluntary control over his socially constituted communicative abilities, to act on the psychological level of deliberately communicating with his mother. Crying itself has two natural functions, that of attracting the mother's attention and of communicating to her that the child wants something. Thus it may be expected that both these functions will become intramental categories for the child: that through continued interactions the child will develop deliberate control of his crying which comes to have two values for him, that of attracting attention, and that of communicating the meaning *want*.

In other words the child and his mother develop a shared and common perception of his activities where initially there was none. From the point of view of the act-structures constituted by the mother's perception of her child's actions it could be said that in his development the child may be expected to internalize them: whereas to begin with the act-structures which his actions create exist on the intermental level, they later come to exist at the intramental level.

Can such developments in the fate of crying be observed in the course of the child's general development? To answer this it becomes necessary to look for examples of the child using crying in the following ways: firstly, it must give evidence of being under voluntary control—can the child, for example, stop crying very quickly? Secondly, it should eventually be used by the child in the pursuit of intended goals: i.e. if it is being used deliberately by him with the value "*want*", he should give some evidence that he knows what he wants. Thirdly, it has to show evidence of deliberate communicative intent: crying may be part of a deliberate attempt to obtain some environmental change, but for it to be of communicative status that change must be attempted by addressing the action to the mother and not the object. The child must attempt to be successful indirectly, through using the mother's agency, and not directly by attempting to employ his own.

Observation 26

Mary; age 10 (16): Mary is sitting on mother's lap playing with a clock. She shakes it very vigorously.

Mother: No, let's put it back.

She takes it from Mary and places it back on the mantlepiece. Mary starts crying, and continues to do so while her mother talks.

Mother: What's the matter? What's the matter?

What do you want?

What is it that you want? Is it this?

Whereupon mother reaches out, picks up the clock and brings it back towards Mary. Mary's crying turns into laughter as mother picks it up.

Mother: Is it this? Yes it is.

Observation 27

Paul; age 9 (26): Paul is sitting on the floor when mother comes in with a pot of tea. She pours a cup for me and herself, then she sits down and starts to read a magazine. Paul starts crying.

Mother: Oh, you, you're an addict.

She puts down the magazine, leans over towards him. Paul stops crying and mother gives him a drink from her cup.

Observation 28

Mary; age 9 (8): Mary is sitting on the floor while mother and I are having a conversation. During this conversation Mary starts making whimpering noises which get louder and louder.

Mother (to me): She's only trying to get some attention.

Mary cries loudly. Mother turns to her and they establish eye contact. Mary smiles.

Mother: It's OK, I haven't forgotten you.

Mary laughs and becomes quiet.

Observation 29

Mary; age 9 (9): Mary is alone. She cries very loudly. Mother rushes in and Mary laughs and smiles at her.

Mother: Oh, you little tyke, you gave me a shock. I thought you were hurt, and you just want to see me!

Observation 30

Peter; age 10 (29): Peter has been enclosed in his playpen for half-an-hour. He tries to reach a brick outside the bars but cannot reach it. He stops his attempts and starts grizzling, this reaching a crescendo when mother comes into the room. He then starts screaming.

Mother: It's no good screaming, you'll have to stay there a bit longer till I've
    finished.
Peter continues screaming until mother leaves the room, when he tails off back
into grizzling.

This group of observations indicates that the child's use of crying does
develop to the stage where it can be said to be used for the purpose of
intentional communication.

The problems of whether crying may be (a) under voluntary control
and (b) be used with knowledge may be considered together, since they
are conceptually interdependent. The fact that crying terminates at
particular instances in these interactive episodes suggests firstly that it
is under voluntary control and, secondly, that the child has some
conception of what he is trying to accomplish by crying. His needs are
now determinate: he can remember them, recognize them, and has
ways of satisfying them. All this constitutes his knowledge. For example, in Observation 26, Mary stops crying when mother begins to pick
up the clock; in Observations 28 and 29 when some attention is directed
at her. Similarly Paul in Observation 27 stops crying when his mother
makes as if to give him some tea. These examples suggest that immediately the child can perceive some relevant change in the environment
he can anticipate "satisfaction" and thus stops crying: that his crying is
under voluntary control, is purposive, and is used with knowledge of its
effects.

Is it aimed or directed at the mother? In Observation 30, Peter's
crying increases in intensity when his mother appears and decreases
when she leaves; in Fig. 6.2 Mary directs her crying to her mother who
is out of the room; in Observation 28, Mother turns her attention to
Mary who is crying, and *immediately* establishes eye contact, i.e. the cry
is being directed at the mother. These episodes suggest that crying *is*
aimed at the mother, the child has some expectations about her subsequent behaviour, and some knowledge of the relationship that objectively exists between his crying and that behaviour.

These observations, and the sequence described in Chapter 2 of the
developments that occur in "frustrated hiccupping", show three facets
of crying: firstly, crying to communicate the meaning *want*; secondly, to
attract the mother's attention apparently *per se*; and thirdly, to perform
both functions at the same time, to both attract attention and convey
the meaning *want*. All three of these functions can be seen in the
following observation, which also illustrates the child's voluntary con-

trol of crying, it being aimed at the mother, and knowledge of what it is that is wanted.

Observation 31
Mary; age 10 (16): Mary has just finished the main part of her dinner. She always has fruit next. Mother is in the pantry getting a banana. Mary cries very loudly while mother is out of sight.
Mother: All right, it won't be long.
Mary cries again.
Mother emerges from the pantry and now has to prepare the banana for Mary.
Mother: It won't be a minute. Do you want a drink? There you are.
She picks up drink and gives it to Mary. Mary stops crying and starts drinking. She puts it down and starts grizzling, looking at mother.
Mother: OK it won't be long.
Mary's grizzles get louder.
Mother: I'll be as quick as I can.
The grizzles get louder still.
Mother: Here you are, now shut up.
She places the banana in front of Mary, who stops crying, picks up her spoon and begins trying to eat.

This observation may be interpreted in the following way. Mary's crying is an instance of her deliberately using for the purpose of communication an item of her behavioural repertoire that was previously only perceived as if it were merely that of making a crying noise, even though it patently was not. Her crying is aimed at her mother—she cries louder when her mother is not there, when she does not have her mother's attention; at other times she is looking at the mother. Her crying is under voluntary control, she terminates it very quickly when given the banana. Finally, she cries with a knowledge of what she is crying about; she does not fully accept a drink, but continues her efforts until given the banana. In terms of the structure of this communicative act, both Mary and her mother perceive Mary's actions with the same value—*want*; and both of them are able to use the context of the crying in the same way, both know what Mary wants. At this stage in her development she is able to use her crying in this way in many different contexts. She has developed the ability to attract her mother's attention and communicate to her that she *wants* something by her behaviour, and is further capable of using the context in which she acts to convey what that something is. Crying can be used deliberately to make a *relationship* determinate.

There is a marked contrast between Laurent and Lucienne's use of crying noted by Piaget (1951; see Chapter 2) at the age of three to four months, and its use above by Peter, Paul and Mary at nine or ten months. Through continual immersion in social interaction the child's action of crying is reflected back to him, and thus his knowledge of crying and how it may be successfully employed is constituted. Crying functions first on the intermental level; but because it does so, and because of the child's innate nature, it finally becomes functional on the intramental level.

4.1.2 Pointing

The three children above also developed actions which functioned within a communicative act in the opposite way to crying: where crying makes a relationship determinate and the context performs a similar function with respect to the object being related to, *pointing,* on the other hand, does the opposite. Pointing functions to make some object determinate, and in this case leaves the context to delineate for the perceiver of the child's actions why the object is being pointed at. Although its actual origins are unimportant, pointing *appears* to arise from unsuccessful direct attempts by the child to grasp or reach for an object, and is transformed by the mother's perception of intentions in the child's reaching and her subsequent actions upon her perceptions. For example, in the following observations, the mother completes the intention she sees behind her child's actions, and in so doing creates for them a potential communicative function.

Observation 32
Mary; age 7 (27): Mary is in her chair, having finished her afternoon meal. Mother comes in through the door with a packet of biscuits in her hand. The door is behind Mary and out of her view. As mother comes in Mary coos and smiles, turning round to see mother.
Mother: Yes, you heard me coming, didn't you?
She enters Mary's field of view, and Mary reaches out towards her mother's hand; her whole body straining in the chair.
Mother: Yes, they're your favourites, aren't they?

Observations 33
Mary; age 9 (6): Mary is being spoon-fed her dinner, and between mouthfuls she cries and bangs the table. Her crying becomes louder and louder.
Mother: No, you can't have your spoon yet (Mary prefers to attempt to feed herself).

Mary continues crying, and attempts to grasp the spoon at the next opportunity.
Mother: No!
Marys spits out her food and reaches again towards the spoon.
Mother: No! That's naughty!
Mary refuses the next spoonful of food, turning her head from the spoon and wriggling, but still reaching out towards it, trying to grasp it.
Mother: All right, you can have it; here you are.
She gives Mary the spoon.

Observation 34
Paul; age 9 (26) (this observation was immediately preceded by Observation 27 above): Paul has his mother's attention, and he reaches out towards the tea-cup. Mother gives him another sip.

Observation 35
Peter; age 9 (18): Peter is sitting on the floor playing with some toys, and Mother is next to him. He stops what he is doing and reaches out towards his toy dog. Mother picks it up and gives it to him. He throws it away.

In all four cases the child's attempt appears to be a direct one, he tries to obtain the object: if the action is intentional then the intention is to grasp the object. Not only is the arm extended, but the child's whole body is involved in a move towards the object. The child fails because the object is too far away. The mother acts to complete what she perceives as the child's intention. Vygotsky (1966: 42–43) proposes an account very similar to that developed above:

> The child tries to grasp too distant an object, but its hand reaching for the object remains hanging in the air and the fingers make grasping movements; this situation [may be] the point of departure for the entire subsequent development. Here for the first time arises the pointing movement which we may with good reason conditionally call a pointing gesture in itself. Here is only the child's movement objectively pointing at the object and nothing else. When the mother comes to the aid of the child and comprehends his movement as a pointing gesture the situation essentially changes. The pointing gesture becomes a gesture for others. The child's unsuccessful grasping movement gives rise to a reaction not from the object, but from another person. The original meaning to this unsuccessful grasping movement is thus imparted by others. And only afterwards, on the basis of the fact that the child associates the unsuccessful grasping movement with the entire objective situation, does the child himself begin to treat this movement as a pointing gesture. Here the

function of the movement itself changes: from a movement directed toward an object it becomes a movement directed toward another person, a means of communication; the grasping is transformed into a pointing .... The child is [however] the last to realise his own gesture. Its meaning and function are created first by the objective situation and then by the people surrounding the child. Thus, the pointing gesture first begins to indicate by movement that which is understood by others and only later becomes a pointing gesture for the child himself.

By acting upon the child's actions the mother creates a social value for them. The child comes to a perception of the values his actions are accorded, and begins to use those actions deliberately.

As a result of the values that are given to these unsuccessful direct attempts at grasping an object, two things may be expected of their subsequent development. Firstly, they will cease to be direct attempts, they will become vestigial and stylized; secondly, and consequently, they will be aimed at obtaining the object through their influence on the mother. That they become vestigial can be seen in Fig. 4.2. At six

Fig. 4.2. Pointing replacing direct grasping of distal objects. *Left,* Mary, age 6 (15): direct grasping. *Right,* Mary, age 12 (20): pointing. (Drawings from video-tape.)

months of age, Mary may be seen making a direct attempt to obtain an object beyond her grasp, her whole body leaning toward the object. But at one year old, by contrast, she is in fact leaning away from the object she indicates. Likewise, in the following observations Mary's reaching towards the object is stylized, her arm is extended in the object's direction in quite a lazy fashion:

Observation 36
Mary; age 10 (13): Mary has had her drink (of tea) for a long time, and it has

gone cold. She now seems more interested in playing with the beaker than drinking from it, and is manipulating it, apparently aimlessly.

Mother: It's not very hot, this, is it? Would you like some more?

Mary grizzles.

Mother: Would you like some more, only hotter? All right. Let's see what we can do.

Mother goes to the other side of the kitchen to prepare a new drink. Mary remains exceptionally quiet, but watches mother, and reaches out her hand towards her.

Mother: Oh, It's not ready yet. Do you want a biscuit? A biscuit?

She gives Mary a biscuit, and continues preparing the drink. Mary eats it while watching her mother.

Observation 37

Mary; age 10 (13): Mary has nearly finished her dinner, her dish is empty, she has been feeding herself and consequently there is a lot of food on the floor. She waves her spoon about and drops it as well. Mother starts cleaning the floor up, during which time Mary attempts eating bread and butter. Mother straightens up and Mary reaches out toward her.

Mother: No, you have this one (picking up a spoon from the table) as this one's been on the floor.

Concrete evidence that this action is aimed at the mother or another agent is rather more difficult to find. The change in the form of the child's behaviour could conceivably be independent of his coming to "aim" the gesture at his mother. Unlike crying, pointing cannot both convey a message and simultaneously attract the mother's attention: it is only effective if the child has the mother's attention. Given, however, that at this stage in the child's development crying is being aimed at the mother, it seems that pointing will be likewise. All these developments can be seen in the following three observations of Paul in separate but very similar situations:

Observation 38

Paul; age 12 (28): Mother leaves the room, placing her cup of tea on the mantelpiece. Paul crawls to the grate and tries to pull himself up. He fails. He then attempts to reach the cup by stretching, and again he fails. He cries in frustration and thus attracts my attention. As I walk over to help him he turns to me, and then strives to reach the cup again. I take it from the mantelpiece and give it to him.

Observation 39

Paul; age 13 (20): The physical situation is again as in Observation 38: Mother has left, leaving her cup of tea on the mantelpiece. Paul crawls to the mantelpiece and cries prior to making an attempt at attaining anything. His cry attracts my attention and we establish eye contact.

A: What's the matter now?

Paul reaches up towards the teacup and turns to look back at me.

Observation 40

Paul; age 14 (23): The situation is exactly the same as above, mother has just left the room leaving her cup of tea on the mantelpiece. Paul crawls directly to me, pulls himself up, turns to look at the mantelpiece and points towards the cup. He turns back to look at me but continues to point to the cup.

In all these cases it is obvious that Paul wants the teacup. Again in all cases he succeeds in attracting my attention, and he performs practically the same actions towards the cup. Similarly in each case the goal of his activities is to obtain the cup of tea, and he is unequivocally pursuing this goal intentionally. Yet with all these similarities, the three observations are not equivalent.

In the first example Paul attempts to attain his goal directly: he does not realize that he will be unsuccessful before he starts. I only become implicated in his activity when he finds his own endeavours are frustrated (in point of fact I only view his cry as one of frustration because of the context his activity has created). Paul has made no attempt to employ his behaviour intentionally for communicative purposes. That he is able to communicate is not a function of his abilities, but a function of my presence, and my ability to make sense of his activities.

In the second observation Paul's cry is made *before* he attempts any direct action in pursuit of his goal, before he fails, and places himself in a "frustrating" situation. He seemingly cries *in order to* obtain my attention and assistance—his cry *is* directed at me since we establish eye contact immediately. What began as an adjustive response to an event ends up as a deliberate attempt to bring about that event.

The third of these observations indicates that Paul does act with knowledge of his situation and not just in a mechanical, conditioned way: he is able to employ other means for attracting my attention for the same end. Further, it is now possible to attribute to pointing or "vestigial reaching" an undoubtedly intentional communicative aspect: it is used to single out *what* Paul wants done after he has made it apparent that he wants something done. The child not only uses crying with the value *want*, and pointing with the value *that*, but both of them also with an understanding that what he is communicating *can only be realized through the actions of another.*

4.2 Contextual determination

Having looked at how actions begin to acquire shared values, it is necessary to consider the other component of the communicative act, its context. If communication is to occur and be meaningful to both participants then not only must the actions used between them have a common value, but both must also share an understanding of the situation in which these actions are used.

No action is performed in a vacuum: it must occur somewhere and at some time, i.e. in some environment. To say that the environment in which an action is performed is its context, is by definition true; but this can only be an illuminating statement if some *objective* description of that environment can be given. It is very difficult to do this when dealing with a *social* environment: a social environment necessarily exists *subjectively*, it is the perceiver who defines his environment. For example, a man may open a factory in an economically depressed area: one action. One group of the community may see his action as laudable in bringing much needed work to the area, another as the exploitation of a cheap work-force: two contexts. The situation between a mother and her child is similar: one action made by either of them is seen from two different viewpoints, seen in two different contexts. How is it possible, beginning from two differing initial viewpoints, to produce a shared context of communication?

The first point that can be made is that *the initial context within which the child acts is created as an* a priori *to his acting.* For example, the child's existence as a biological individual creates the value of "food" for certain objects. Secondly, other actions will immediately take on values in the cultural world he has been born into, as evidenced by Macfarlane's study (1974, 1977) of the interpretations mothers give to the activities of their new-born infants; e.g. "he's just showing off".

The mother seems to treat her child from three different standpoints: from what she knows of the child, firstly as *a* child and secondly as *her* child; and thirdly in the light of what she *intends* for her child. The first of these standpoints has effectively been discussed above—the mother can interpret the child's actions because she sees them in a context created by her knowledge of infants in general. This could very crudely be termed placing the infant in his biological context. An example of the second standpoint can be seen in Fig. 4.3. At this time Mary is in the "habit" of picking up small objects and placing them in her mouth: a habit which the mother is trying to break. In this example, Mary turns away from looking at the camera (1-3) and adjusts her position (4-5). In making this adjustment she moves her head such that a piece of fluff on the floor comes into her field of view, and at the same time this fact is noticed by the mother (6). Because of her knowledge of Mary's "habit"

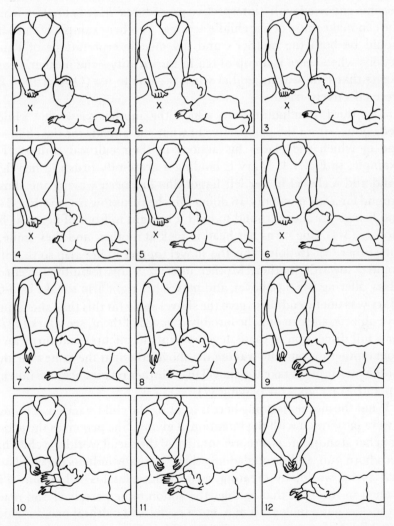

Fig. 4.3. Mary, age 6 (15): mother anticipating child's action—see text. (Drawing from video-tape.)

and her intentions to put a stop to it, the mother reaches out and removes the fluff just as Mary begins moving her right arm (7-9). Mary completes her action (10-12) but the fluff has already gone.

Here the mother is capable of acting so effectively because of her intimate knowledge of *her* child. The context within which Mary acts is one that has been created by her previous actions; similarly the knowledge the mother has of her child has been created within the dyad. Through transactions between the mother and child the mother has become endowed with "interpretive procedures" (see below) by which she can make sense of her child's actions. Another example of this kind would be both the mother's and my own interpretations of Paul's actions when there is a cup of tea in the vicinity—the mother's comments that Paul was an addict when it came to tea (Observation 27) were effectively true.

The third standpoint from which the mother views her child's behaviour—from the perspective of what she intends for the child—is one in which she places his actions in their cultural context. For example, in Fig. 4.4. Mary is holding a grate-tidy brush in her right hand and a shovel in her left hand. She has been waving the shovel around for a few moments. In doing this she turns towards mother (1-2) and brings the shovel round to hold it upright in front of her near her mother (3-4). She turns her head to look at mother, and they smile at each other (5). In doing this the shovel topples in her grip so that it is pointed towards mother. Mother interprets this fortuitous event as Mary offering her the shovel, and moves her right arm to take it (5-6). Mary was not intending to give the shovel away (at this time she cannot give objects, she can only be forcibly relieved of them, see Clark (1978) for a full discussion of these developments in infants) and turns away from mother to continue waving the shovel about at the same time that mother attempts to take the shovel (6). Mother relaxes her arm into her lap and Mary goes on playing (7).

What the mother is doing here is treating the child's action as though it were performed with the intention of giving. She perceives the action from her standpoint as a representative of the social world the child has been born into, and through doing this eventually inducts the child into that social world, by creating social values for his behaviour. The context in this case that enables the action to be perceived and made sense of is not a biological one, but a social and cultural one, in which the child does not as yet participate. The above examples have been concerned with how the mother is able to use contextual information of

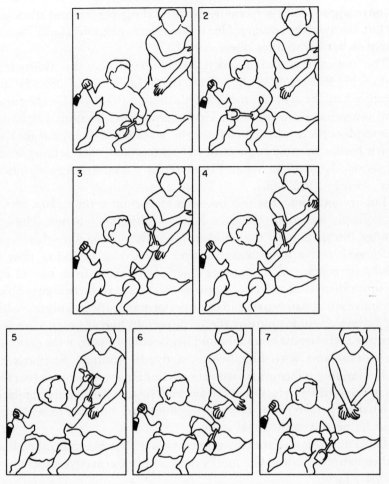

Fig. 4.4. Mary, age 6 (15): mother "reading beyond" Mary's actions–see text. (Drawings from video-tape.)

three different sorts—biological, dyadic and cultural—to make sense of the child's behaviour.

Turning now to the child: recall that an integral aspect of the process of need-determination discussed in the previous chapter is its effect upon the perceptions an organism has of the outside world. Not only does the child come to a structured perception of his own inner experiences through this process, he also comes to perceive the material world in a structured way with respect to his concrete bodily needs. These perceptions can now function to inform his actions such that he can perform appropriate behaviour. Further, these perceptions illuminate for him many of the actions of his mother, he can "understand" to some extent, what his mother does.

The first context within which the child evidences this ability is the biological. Piaget (1952: 60) notes that "Lucienne at 0;3(12) stops crying when she sees her mother unfastening her dress for the meal". This is a prime example of the kind of ability in question. The child is able to place the mother's behaviour in relation to a biological goal with which he has become cognizant, to "understand" her actions, and to consequently react in what Piaget terms "a completely significant way" (Piaget, 1952: 60).

The second context which becomes important is the dyadic one. As an example we could consider Paul's "addiction" to tea. Here the mother interacts with the child in a consistent fashion where tea is concerned over a long period of time. Over this period of time the child's perception of his mother's actions changes from one of total uncomprehension to a very complete one. In short, he becomes able to recognize earlier and earlier in their performance the intentions behind the mother's actions: putting the kettle on tells him as much as seeing a cup of tea. He begins to understand her behaviour within the context of her interactions with him, within a dyadic context. Similarly this understanding informs his own actions: he can now perform his actions not in the world as it is, but in the world as he sees it: not only in relation to what he perceives the mother *is* going to do, but also in relation to what he perceives she *ought* to do.

This conception of socially agreed values that maintain the child's ability to act is akin to Cicourel's notion of "interpretive procedures" (1973) which

> provide the actor with a developmentally changing sense of social struc-
> ture that enables him to assign meaning or relevance to an environment of
> objects.   (1973: 30)

The acquisition of these "interpretive procedures" has another important aspect, in that it

> provides the actor with a basis for assigning meaning to his environment
> or a sense of social structure, thus orienting him to the relevance of
> "surface rules" or "norms".   (1973: 45)

When looking at the child younger than seven months or so, one is looking at the establishment of basic values such that the child can see his own endeavours as meaningful. Once this occurs he is able to shift the form of his behaviour so that it comes to take a culturally acceptable form, or a skilful one, i.e. he acquires the "surface rules" that produce an acceptable performance. This "shift" is a service that must be rendered by another who is in possession of the "surface rules" that prescribe "acceptability" (cf. Shotter, 1974a). Thus the child comes to perform his actions in a third context—the cultural one.

These transitions from one context to another can be followed in the case of crying. Firstly, the child has no interpretive structures whatsoever, but quite quickly gains some which operate within a biological context: an example of this being Piaget's (1952) report on Laurent and Lucienne. Next the child moves into the social context, gaining interpretive procedures with respect to social events. Thus he is able to use his crying deliberately with the value *WANT*. Finally he must learn the culturally sanctified surface rules prescribed for the expression of this value. The cry must take the form of a word. This appears to occur, crying metamorphosing into *mama* (see Chapter 7). Similarly, instead of pointing he begins to name objects. Through the further creative interpretations his parents give to his single-word utterances, that surface-structure is further refined from "baby-talk" to the adult form.

There are, then, a number of important reasons for looking at the construction of goals within the dyad: these shared goals create the *contexts* in which crying and pointing are often used. Further, these goals endow the child with interpretive procedures, also serve to orient him to surface rules. In learning to pursue these goals the form of the child's behaviour may be seen to change, so that it comes to be a socially acceptable performance.

4.3 The construction and pursuit of dyadic goals

Three examples of goal construction are considered here. In all three cases the so-called interpretive procedures arise in the same way, but the surface rules governing the performance develop differently. These three examples are: Paul learning to kick; Mary learning to play with interlocking cups; and Mary again, learning to feed herself.

4.3.1 Learning to kick

Observation 41
Paul; age 12 (16): Paul is just starting to walk with assistance. His mother

stands behind him holding his upstretched arms and supporting him while he totters forward. He does not look at his feet but straight ahead. A football is on the floor in their path. Paul does not look at it, but it is inevitable that he is going to kick it or fall over it if he keeps going in the same direction.

Mother: There's your football, kick it, kick it, go on, kick it.

They continue walking and Paul's right foot hits the ball as it swings forward.

Paul's attention is caught by the movement and he laughs as he watches the ball move away.

Mother: Oh, aren't you clever. Shall we do it again? Come on you, kick it
         again. Come on, kick it,

and she turns them both round so that they are moving towards the ball again. Paul stumbles into it and the ball rolls away catching his attention again. He laughs.

Mother: Oh there's a clever boy, did you kick it, aren't you good.

Observation 42
Paul; age 12 (22): I have not seen Paul since the time of the above observation. He crawls over to where I am sitting, pulls himself up and then edges along in an upright position holding the settee.

A: Do you want some proper practice, come on,

and I take his hands, turn him round and get ready to help him walk. Last week (above) he was not at all proficient at this, very tottery, and the direction in which he went was determined by the person holding him from above and behind. Further, he did not look down towards the floor, but always straight ahead. Today, however, he looks around the floor before we set off. I try and go in a straight line, but Paul pulls hard to my right, keeping his head down. I turn to go in that direction and find the football is three or four steps in front of us. Paul practically drags me towards it and then kicks it, laughs and watches it. It bounces off a chair and rolls behind us. Paul twists to keep it in view and pulls in that direction. I hold him and follow, whereupon he kicks it again. He laughs. Mother enters from the kitchen and laughs as well.

Between these two observations the mother reported that they have played football every day, and that Paul is getting better at it. During this period something that occurred purely as an accident has been elevated to the position of a goal that can be intentionally pursued. This has been done primarily by the mother setting the accident as a goal to be attained, and contriving to guide the child in continually producing that accident. In aiding Paul's walking the mother has invariably created a mutually enjoyable event where he bangs the football in the process of moving his feet. She further manages to concentrate his attention away from his attempts at walking, at which he is continually improving, and on to the football. She thus sets up a situation of walking towards something that Paul has his attention on and then creating an event which is mutually satisfactory. Paul transforms the motive force by which the football is moved from an accidental "kick" to a deliberate kick during this time, and secondly becomes less and less dependent upon his mother for guiding him to the football—he can locate it and orientate himself upon it. Thus he learnt to play football.

This example provides an exceptionally clear instance of Vygotsky's dictum (1962) "in order to subject a function to intellectual and volitional control we must first possess it". The *whole* sequence is performed unintentionally in the first instance. Ignoring the mother's part, Paul moves towards the football, collides with it, watches it roll away and laughs in both cases: at this level both instances are similar. The only level at which they differ is that of intention. In the first instance the mother intentionally guides Paul's behaviour; in the second he guides himself.

Now while this example gives a very clear indication of how a goal is established to function as an interpretive procedure, it is not illuminating in terms of negotiated aspects of goal creation and the acquisition of surface structures. This is because the goal established is very simple, and in terms of execution, very stringent: there is effectively only one way of accomplishing the task. The surface rules determining the acceptability of the attempted performance are necessarily constituted by the nature of the task, and not by social agreement. In the next example the concern is again with the acquisition of an ability in the context of a relatively circumscribed activity. The nature of the task to be performed structures in advance what will constitute an acceptable performance, but the task is more intricate than the above one. Consequently it functions as a bridge between the first example and the final quite complex one.

4.3.2 Learning to play with cups

Mary has been given a set of ten brightly coloured cups of differing size which fit into each other. The nature of the toy concretely structures the way Mary is expected to play with it. At the time she is given it, however, this way is far beyond her abilities. Thus firstly the mother has to teach her the goal, and secondly Mary has to learn how to do it.

Observation 43
Mary; age 6 (23): Mary is sitting on the floor, with her mother sitting in front of her with the cups. This is the first time Mary has seen them.

Mother: What are these then. Ooh, look, aren't they pretty. (She starts taking
           them apart.) Look, here's a little green one, and a red one, and a blue
           one. Oh aren't they pretty.
Mary does not appear in the least bit interested.
Mother: And look, they all fit together, that one, then this one, then this one
           and . . . here, you have one.
She places a cup in Mary's lap. Mary pats it and then picks it up and sucks it.
She then bangs it on the floor and lets go of it so that it bounces away from her.
Mother: Do you want another one, do you, here you are.
Mary repeats her previous performance.

In this interaction the mother has demonstrated the goal, and found
that she is not going to be very successful in getting Mary to attain it for
a long time. Consequently she may be found employing new strategies
and pursuing new intentions around such interactions.

By the time Mary is aged 9 (7) there are basically three strategies
operating with the cups. Mary's play with them has developed in line
with the schemas she has come to possess. Typically she will remove a
cup from the stack, immediately take another, and then bang them
together. She will then throw one away, pick up another and repeat the
above. If instead of picking up a new one she is offered one by her
mother she usually drops the one she already has before taking the one
offered. It is at this level that one of the mother's interactive strategies
operates—the erection of goals which are within the child's mental
grasp—i.e. playing at the child's level of ability. The other two
strategies are playing above the child's level, but within the constraints
of the task, and playing beyond the confines of the task.

(a) Playing at the child's level

Observation 44
Mary; age 9 (7): Mary is sitting on the floor, playing with two cups, banging
them together. Mother joins her, picks another cup up and offers it to her.
Mother: Do you want this one? Here you are.
Marys drops the cup in her left hand and reaches out to take the proffered one.
She grasps it and bangs it against the one she still has. Mother retrieves the
discarded one.
Mother: Here, bang this one, no don't take it but bang it, come on.
She starts to bang it against the one in Mary's right hand. Mary drops it and
takes the one from her mother.
Mother: No silly, like this,
and she attempts to repeat the above, but has little success.

As can be seen there is little attempt to go beyond Mary's present abilities. The attempt at innovation by the mother remains at the same level, and merely attempts to broaden the sphere of their application. Should Mary learn to do what her mother wants her to she will establish interpretive procedures and surface rules at the same time.

(b) Play aimed at progressing to a new level within the task

Observation 45
Mary; age 9 (7): Mary is sitting on the floor between her mother and a neighbour. Mother picks up the cups that are scattered around.
Mother: Come on, you show us what you can do.
Mother starts putting the cups together.
Mother: Look, there they go, all together.
Mary looks blank and disinterested.
Neighbour: She said you can do what you like with them, I'm not bothered.
Mother: Look, Mary, it's gone, look, I've only got one left. (She tips them up on the floor.) Ah, there they all are.
Mother starts to repeat, Mary turns round and starts crawling towards the television. At present she likes to play with all the wires and plugs near it.
Mother: No. No!
I take her away from that area.
A: I think she's showing you up, not showing you off.

Mary's mother rarely became involved in such demonstrative situations. Mary cannot put the cups together, and thus the mother's demonstration is probably meaningless to her. It is only by *actively* involving Mary in the situation that the mother is able to create certain events as significant for her. This example does, however, make two points explicit. Firstly, its atypicality was occasioned by the neighbour's presence: a proud mother tries to "show off" her child. Secondly, there is the neighbour's natural reaction to construe Mary's lack of interest into her own terms: "I'm not bothered . . .". She is doing what all people do with babies, treating Mary anthropomorphically: making verbally explicit what is implicit in the child's behaviour.

(c) Irrelevant play, or pure play, in which there exists the possibility of inventing new goals that are not laid down by the task structure

In this example there first occurs play of the second category—interactive extension of Mary's abilities—and secondly pure play.

Observation 46

Mary; age 9 (7): Mary, mother and I are sitting in a circle. Mary is banging two cups together. In doing this she accidentally pushes one inside the other and loses her grip on it. She looks startled and gazes at her empty hand.

Mother: Oh, there's a clever girl, where's it gone? Look, here it is.

She takes Mary's empty hand and places it inside the two cups.

Mother: There it is, pull, pull.

Mary's fist is jammed in the cup, and as mother pulls her arm back the lost cup emerges. Mary watches and laughs.

Mother: Look, there it is, push it back.

She pushes Mary's arm and the cup slides back, Mary watches and laughs. She frees her hand from mother's grip and grasps the edge of the cup, pulling it out. She waves it in the air.

Mother: Yes, aren't you clever? What is it? (She takes the cup from Mary.) Mummy have it on her head—Andy have one on his head, and you have one on your head. That's it, we all sit like idiots now.

The cup falls off mother's head onto the floor with a bang. Mary looks and smiles and mother laughs.

A: You've got one as well.

Mary looks at me, and then at the top of my head. The cup falls off and she watches it, laughs and looks back at me. In doing this her own cup falls off, but she pays no attention to this. Mother puts a cup back on her own head and Mary stares at her with wide open eyes and mouth. The game continues without Mary joining in the action until it degenerates into raucous laughter.

The pure play portion of this sequence contains the possibility of being elevated to the level of a ritual, or significant event. If this is to occur then it requires some activity on Mary's part. Had she responded with enthusiasm, for example, the game would have continued, consolidating that behaviour within her repertoire as a procedure to make interesting sights last, and erecting the game as a significant event. The importance of these possibilities for such play will be seen later when discussing the learning of words. The next development in this context is as follows:

Observation 47

Mary; age 11 (5): Mary has two cups and is pushing them together.

Mother: No, you won't do it that way. Here, try this one instead.

She takes the one Mary is trying to fit into the other and replaces it with a much smaller one.

Mother: There, now try again.
Mary does and it fits.

What Mary first achieved as an accident has become interactively constructed as a goal for her to aim at. Her efforts have been concentrated in this direction through the play situation being actively focused by the mother on the attainment of this ability. She has not yet discovered the appropriate actions to accomplish this easily, nor has she realized that the relative size of the cups is important. Her next development is to make this size discrimination, always attempting to put the smaller into the larger, her success then being frustrated by her lack of manual dexterity. When this develops, it can be seen that in interactions around this game the dyad members have become equals:

Observation 48
Mary; age 12 (7): Mary is fitting two cups of near equal size together.
Mother: Look, you've got that the wrong way, it'll have to go like . . .
She starts to reach out to do this for her when Mary adjusts the relative positions of the cup and completes the task.

Mary now shows that after 170 days of being involved in interactive situations focusing on playing with these cups she is capable of perceiving her immediate situation in the same way as her mother. She has gained an equivalent knowledge of what she is doing, and in this instance she can perceive, with an ability equal to the mother's, what must be done next.

4.3.3 Learning to eat

Unlike the above two tasks, the situation in question here is unstructured by the substrates on which the dyad must act: there is no correct way of attaining the goal given by the nature of the task, just many equivalent possible ways. Thus in the establishment of an ultimate strategy for pursuing this goal there can be seen not the discovery of the way things *must* be done due to physical constraints, but the construction by interactive negotiated agreement of a way in which things *may* be done due to social constraints.

When weaning occurs, a problem arises as to how the child will be fed. At weaning the child's hand—mouth co-ordination is generally well established, and he could conceivably feed himself. The way in which food passes from plate to mouth is, however, an area in which social convention is strongly established. One reason why we laugh so heartily at a chimpanzee's tea party is its total lack of etiquette: the object of such an event for the chimp is to eat as much as possible, as quickly as possible, with no restraints. Young children would doubtless eat in the same way, and often attempt to do so, were it not for someone placing limits on the activity, setting up rules as to what is permissible and what is not when it comes to table manners.

The way in which the infant comes to feed himself is reached by a process of negotiation in which the level of the child's skills is traded off against the limits of the mother's tolerance. Thus there is no regular progression between the child's discovery of the unsocialized goal—placing food in the mouth—and the attainment of the socialized goal—eating with a knife and fork, but a series of negotiated and continually changing sublevels of functioning, steadily moving from the asocial to the social mode. The mother sets up the act-structures within which they will operate, e.g. she decides when he will use a spoon, but she does not predetermine how the child will *initially* use the spoon. They negotiate the performance of the act at the action level in terms of what the child can actually do, what the mother will allow him to do, and, often, what the child will allow the mother to do.

In certain cases the mother will not tolerate the mess that is inevitable in the child's early attempts at feeding himself, and so he is not allowed to until he is about two or more years old. Other mothers will put up with a quite staggering amount of muckiness, and consequently the child is allowed to start quite young. In this sequence it is possible to observe how the mother's tolerance changes, and how by doing this she "teaches" her child to feed herself. Initially Mary's mother is excited by Mary's early attempts to feed herself, and encourages them. In doing this she tolerates a lot of mess. As Mary grows older, she becomes less tolerant and so forces Mary to adopt a more "social" way of feeding herself. As Mary becomes better at using a spoon, the way in which she must use it becomes more and more constrained. While Mary's ability develops continually, the mother's tolerance changes abruptly. This means that the child can never stagnate at one level of functioning.

Observation 49
Mary; age 6 (15): Mary is passively spoon-fed. Her control over the rate at which she is fed is confined to turning her head from the proffered spoon, and if the mother does not respond to this, to undirected waving and gross bodily

wriggling. On this occasion in waving her arms about Mary effectively pushes the spoon away, her hand having struck the mother's and the spoon by chance, at the same time.

Mother: Ooh, there's a clever girl, are you going to take the spoon and feed yourself?

Mother moves her hand away to leave Mary holding the spoon alone. She immediately drops it.

Mary's accidental "grasping" of the spoon here is perceived by the mother in a very constructive way. What was an accidental banging of the spoon in waving her arms about is perceived as an attempt to take the spoon in order to feed herself. The mother "wants" to perceive these actions in this way, for she wants to see evidence that her child is "growing up". Further in this case, Mary's mother seemed highly motivated to have Mary feeding herself as quickly as possible through a rivalry with the next-door neighbour whose 18-month-old child could not feed himself at all, his mother not allowing him to try since she would not put up with the associated mess. This readiness to interpret Mary's actions constructively is extremely important in the context of Mary coming to feed herself, *as it opens up the possibility of her doing so prior to her acting*; what Mary's actions make determinate is effectively predetermined. The mother will attempt to use the opportunities presented fortuitously by Mary's actions towards the pursuit of intentions she has formulated in independence of their interaction. In other words, the mother is aware of what she is trying to do here; she tries to teach. This may be seen later again, when she tries deliberately to teach Mary words. Not all mothers are this aware of what they are attempting; they discover many of their intentions retroactively through interaction, or are never even conscious of them.

Observation 50

Mary; age 7 (10): A spoonful of food has just been placed in Mary's mouth when the telephone rings. Mother takes Mary's left hand and wraps it round the spoon handle which is sticking from Mary's mouth.

Mother: You take it while Mummy answers the phone.

Mary pulls the spoon from her mouth and while eating waves it about. While still holding the spoon she pushes her hand around in her dinner, and then starts licking her hand. While she is doing this mother returns.

Mother: There's a clever girl, are you feeding yourself? Here, let's wipe you, you're ever so mucky.

She takes the spoon from Mary to wipe her. Mary cries and struggles, then reaches out towards spoon.
Mother: All right, here you are. Let me show you.
She gives Mary the spoon, and then guiding her hand places it into the dish, and then to Mary's mouth.
Mother: Oh, aren't we clever! Aren't we clever!

Here again the mother seizes on an opportunity that occurs by accident, and perhaps by her reaction to it makes that event take on a significance for the child. Mary rapidly learns to push her spoon around in her dish and then to lick it: she does not learn as quickly how to get food on to the spoon, nor how to orient the spoon correctly to do so. In the next feeding session that was observed (below) the mother may be seen retreating somewhat in her enthusiasm for Mary performing this activity, because of the mess she makes. However, in retreating she starts to break down the task into sub-components and aims to teach Mary step by step.

Observation 51
Mary; age 7 (26): In pushing her spoon around the dish Mary tends to empty the dish rather than fill the spoon. Further, should she manage to get food into the spoon, she rarely manages to transfer it successfully to her mouth: she does not yet hold the spoon in a proper way. As a consequence Mary is no longer allowed to push the spoon around her dish, but only allowed to take it once her mother has filled it. Since she is given the spoon in its correct orientation she can transfer it to her mouth without spilling the food on the floor, but she is not very capable of pushing spoon and food into her mouth at once, and tends to drop the food on to the floor at this time.

Feeding times become rather fractious, as the spoon is continually being taken from Mary to be refilled, and she cries each time this happens. The mother, however, puts up with this. Mary is left to discover for herself how to manipulate and control a food-laden spoon. At this time she cannot do this, and most of the food goes over her rather than in her. As a consequence she is equipped with a new rigid bib containing a slop tray. When her feeding-dish is empty it is refilled from the slops and this process continues until the food is eaten or the mother gets fed up. In an attempt to curtail the time involved in feeding, the mother force-feeds Mary in the early part of the meal to reduce the amount of food to be practised on as much as possible. Mary's resistance to being force-fed grows stronger as the meal continues, and the point at which she is allowed to take over is negotiated at the practical level through a balancing out by the mother of how much food is left, how much noise and fuss Mary is making and how incompetent she is at that time; present noise is traded against future mess. This may be seen below:

Observation 52
Mary; age 9 (8): Mary is being force-fed, but is banging the table and blowing raspberries between spoonfuls, simultaneously attempting to grasp the spoon. Mother battles on. The noise and banging reach a crescendo, and in blowing raspberries she spits out a mouthful of food all over her mother.
Mother: (***)! (Expletive deleted)
Mary: bangs and is noisy.
Mother: No, you can't have your spoon yet.
Mary: bangs louder and is noiser.
Mother: Be quiet, that's naughty!
Mary: spits food out over mother again.
Mother: All right, you can have your spoon! Here it is!

During the period between this observation and the preceding one Mary exhibits more and more frustration at any intervention by her mother, and so she starts to encroach upon the division of labour that has been set up. However, unlike being left to discover and practice getting a spoonful of food into her mouth on her own, she is assisted by direct intervention on the mother's part in learning to get food on to the spoon in the first place. This can be seen below:

Observation 53
Mary; age 10 (15): Mother has fed Mary two mouthfuls and she is already becoming impatient to take the spoon herself. She leans over as mother gets the spoon filled in the bowl and reaches for it.
Mother: Just a min . . . . Oh all right, you hold the spoon, but don't tip it up, do it properly.
Mary holds the spoon and then bangs it down on the table, making a mess.
Mother: Now that was naughty, wasn't it?

As noted, in this food transference task Mary gets no help: in the other task, spoon-filling, she does:

Observation 54
Mary; age 10 (16): Mary is attempting to get pieces of banana onto the spoon from her dish, but finds this difficult. She cries; mother takes her hand.

Mother: Look . . .
and she guides Mary's hand and spoon until a piece of banana is on the spoon.
Mary then lifts it to her mouth.
Mother: That's a clever girl. Are you going to get some more out of the dish?
Mary tries, but is not immediately successful.
Mother: No . . .
She is about to intervene when Mary accomplishes the task.
Mother: Ah, that's it.

From this time the overall strategy of feeding is reversed. Instead of being force-fed first and then allowed to continue on her own, Mary is allowed to feed herself from both her plate and her slop-tray until mother wants to get dinner finished, when she force-feeds Mary what is remaining. Mary resents these interventions:

Observation 55
Mary; age 11 (5): Mary has been left to feed herself while mother does the ironing. Mother returns.
Mother: Have you nearly finished? Is it time for Mummy to come and empty
          your tray? Oh there's a good girl, you're nearly done. Come on, just
          this bit,
and she tries to force-feed Mary, who turns her head away, threshes about and cries.
Mother: Oh, all right, you mardy, I won't stand for that again!
and she takes the food away.

Because of the child's increasing ability to perform this task the mother becomes less and less tolerant of her mistakes and tantrums at not getting her own way. Mary performs so well now that the mother no longer praises her so much, nor allows her extra time to complete the task when that is inconvenient. Thus there emerges a new status quo in which the events that were previously exaggerated by the mother to make them significant have become part of Mary's habits and skilled repertoire which no longer need commenting upon. Mary reaches the stage where she no longer protests at her mother's intervention to terminate a meal. Meals are no longer "fun" but routine: Mary herself seems to want to get them over as quickly as possible in order to get back to playing:

Observation 56
Mary; age 11 (28): Mary is eating pear slices for dessert and has difficulty in getting them on the spoon.

Mother: Can't you get those bits. Mummy help. Give Mummy the spoon. She holds out her hand, but has to take the spoon from Mary. She then feeds Mary the last few pieces without any fuss.

The varied aspects of development discussed in this chapter relate to a common theme. As the child develops he comes to be able to act not only *intelligently*, but also *intelligibly*. He begins to understand his activities in a way he shares with his mother. He is no longer merely perceived to act in such-and-such a fashion, he actually does act in that way. It is within this shared context of action that the child is able to employ the gestures he has developed. The two gestures of most importance here are firstly, crying—which attracts attention and communicates a relationship—and secondly, pointing—which determines the object of some such relationship. These gestures are presently used singly.

5. Semantic force
and implication

The main trend discernible in the development of children's communicative abilities from this point onwards, as outlined in the following chapters, is their progressively decreasing reliance upon contextual completion. Children become able to determine more and more of the content of the messages they send by their own actions, and progressively less information is "carried" by the context in which their actions are performed. The discussion in previous chapters has been related to how, as a result of the mother's actions towards certain portions of her child's behaviour, the child begins to possess and use effectively the actions of, primarily, crying and pointing to communicate and attain his goals. The child at this stage has moved from being perceived to communicate to actually being able to communicate, but in doing so he uses only one of his gestures at a time.

The next development to occur in the sphere of communication is illustrated in Chapter 6: the child begins to use more than one gesture at a time. These gestures have agreed values, and they occur together, as do words in "sentences". There does in fact appear to be a remarkable parallel between the transition from single to multi-gestural use and that from single to multi-word utterances. The transition from gestural usage to word usage (discussed in Chapter 10) suggests a direct correspondence between many communicative acts composed of two gestures and those later composed of two words. The question then arises as to whether it is legitimate to look for the origins of grammar in this gestural stage, in the child's ability to combine gestures: an ability which the child neither learns—where could he learn it from?—nor is driven to by innate programming. But, as Richards (1974a: 91) points out,

> Social communication itself is much more than a simple mutual responsiveness to signals and it involves notions of mutuality, reciprocity and intersubjectivity. One of the greatest problems in attempting to trace the development of this process in the preverbal infant is that all the concepts that have proved so useful in the analysis of adult communication are essentially linguistic.

Thus if "grammar" begins in preverbal non-linguistic communication then "grammatical theory" requires an overhaul; its origins and basis in non-linguistic forms of communication need clarifying. Some of the key concepts required for this overhaul are discussed below.

5.1 Semantic force

The notion I would like to introduce is that of "semantic force": it bears the same relation to Austin's concept of an "illocutionary force" (1962) as "communicative act" bears to Searle's "speech act" (1969): although more general, it retains a great deal of similarity to its conceptual forebears. Austin (1962: 120) distinguishes in language and action four forms of act: "the locutionary act . . . which has a *meaning*; the illocutionary act which has a certain *force* in saying something; the perlocutionary act which is the achieving of certain *effects* by saying something"; and finally the act itself. If Austin's concepts are broadened to include non-linguistic acts, they may be used to shed some light on mother–child interaction: for while the child *may come* to perform non-linguistic acts equivalent to locution and perlocution, he performs the equivalent of illocutionary acts *by nature*.

In introducing the idea of illocutionary acts, Austin notes that:

> for some years we have been realising more and more clearly that the occasion of an utterance matters seriously, and that the words used are to some extent to be explained by the "context" in which they are designed to be or have actually been spoken in a linguistic interchange. Yet still perhaps we are too prone to give these explanations in terms of "the meanings of words".   (1962: 100)

D

The problem Austin is referring to can be illustrated by expanding an example given by Gordon and Lakoff (1971); the sentence "It's stuffy in here". At first sight this sentence appears to be merely a statement. But when used by different speakers it may possess different functions: by a lord to his butler it may mean "Open the window"; by a salesman to a housewife "Why don't you buy our air-freshener"; by a student in an examination, "I am about to faint". The diverse *meanings* of this *locutionary act* constitute what Austin terms the *illocutionary force* of the utterance: its *value through usage* rather than its *abstracted meaning*.

It is quite conceivable that in the above the illocutionary force of the utterance is intended by the speaker. Such forces need not, however, be of this nature. For example, a young child may say, "It's stuffy in here" when to his mother it is not. She thus treats the child's utterance not at the level of the meaning of the words he spoke, but at the level of its illocutionary force: the value she gives it in terms of the context in which it is uttered. That is, she assumes on the basis of it that her child is starting a cold. If it is assumed that the child in question does not know about colds and their symptoms, and is not therefore in this case able to determine his bodily state, the illocutionary force of his utterance was purely unintentional.

By now it must be fairly obvious that something pertaining to an illocutionary force exists within the child's social actions prior to his being able to speak; i.e. the converse of Austin's notion of the performative utterance is (effectively) true: doing certain things is equivalent to saying certain things. It is solely to avoid confusion in the use of terminology that the actions of the child are said to possess a *semantic force,* a force drawn from the acts in which his actions are implicated or in fact constitute. A semantic force may exist in an *act*; an illocutionary force in a speech act.

By adopting a genetico-historical perspective (cf. Sanborn, 1971), the components of any such semantic force may be legitimately restated in terms of an adult speech act, these then representing the "target" for the particular abilities the child may be seen as developing towards. However, the relationships between these components does not arise by reference to the adult form of speech, but from a different source entirely (see Section 5.4). For example, while a child's cry may have no meaning for him, it has a semantic force given by the components of adult speech as I WANT THAT: but the relationships pertaining between the elements of this force do not stem from any grammatical concept or theory which might account for the linguistic realization of this force; to recall Mead here, the roots of such structures are to be found not in the child, nor in his environment, but in the relations between the two.

5.2 The assignment of semantic force: meaning and structure prior to patterned speech

In studying the language development of three young children, Bloom (1970) utilized information from the context in which the child used a word, and the behaviour he was engaged in, for the purpose of inferring the semantic intention behind, and in turn the structure of, that utterance. This tactic has been termed "rich interpretation" by Brown (1973): "quite simply, one infers more about the child's utterance than is possible when one considers only what the child actually says" (quoted by Bloom, 1973: 133). Bloom goes on to note that:

> Since the tactic of "rich" interpretation was, in a sense, "legitimised" (Bloom, 1970; Brown, 1973), a number of other investigators have used it in studying the semantic development of children using single-word utterances—in the period before the use of syntax (Smith, 1970; McNeill, 1970; Greenfield *et al.*, 1972). Their reasoning has gone something like this : if "Mommy pigtail" really means "Mommy verb (me) pigtail", then just "Mommy" or just "pigtail" in the same context, when the child is limited to only one word at a time, must have the same underlying structure. Further, that a child will say the same word in two different situations, for example, the single word "light" when he sees the light and "light" when he wants to turn on the light, provides evidence, in this view, that he knows two different structures or "meanings" corresponding to the two different uses of the word.   (Bloom, 1973: 133–134)

Such a mode of analysis may sound unacceptably subjective but Greenfield *et al.* (1972) argue that this is not in fact the case (pp. 47–53) and give in substantiation of their argument the following example (p. 50):

> a child reaches for an apple and, in a whining voice, says *apple*. The mother might expand this utterance in a number of ways: "Oh, you want an apple", "Oh, you are demanding an apple", "It's an apple you want", or even, to a third person, "John wants an apple". What is common to all these expansions is the semantic structure of the situational elements upon which each is based. That is, John has related himself to the apple

through his reach and his whine. Here, John is the Agent, reaching (and possible whining) the Action, and apple the Object. The verbal element *apple* corresponds to the non-verbal element occupying the role of *object* in this situational structure.

Thus the method of "rich interpretation" is one which is applicable in the case of one-word utterances. But such a method is not by itself sufficient to attribute a knowledge of structural relationships to children who are only capable of using single words, and the other major sources of evidence which are available by syntactic data do not exist during the period (Bloom, 1973: 134–135). Consequently, one is forced to agree with Bloom's conclusion (1973: 137–138) that in the one-word period, although it is apparently possible to use the method of "rich interpretation" to describe how the child uses his words in relation to his situation, one should not attribute linguistic knowledge to him.

However, Ryan (1974: 205), in discussing the views put forward by these more recent writers on child language development, points out that,

> these views of the nature of early speech are essentially interpretive ones, and should more accurately be described as views about how adults understand (or fail to understand) child speech than as views of the speech itself.

And Ryan's argument, although it seems a very negative one, does have an important positive aspect. She is essentially pointing out that mothers have used the tactic of rich interpretation in real-life situations for aeons of time before it fell into the hands of developmental psycholinguists, and in doing this she makes apparent the similarity between this tactic and that of treating the child "as if". This similarity becomes even more striking when a suggestion made by Greenfield *et al.* (1972: 52) is considered:

> the ability of adults to assign semantic structure to the situational context surrounding an utterance could be an important key to the nature of the communication process between a child in the process of learning a language and the mature speaker.

The previous discussion of the development of gestures suggests that this ability is of prime importance in that case as well, that through interpreting the child's actions-in-context the mother is functioning to transform those actions into gestures, and to create simultaneously a value, or semantic structure, for them.

The problem here, then, is that if a mother's "rich interpretation" is responsible for the child developing a shared communicative system— if by treating him in our interactions with him as if he meant such-and-such and in so doing provide him with the materials out of which he can later fabricate the ability to actually mean such-and-such—can the point which the child has reached at any time in this development be determined? The strict answer is no: but this does not mean that no account of his development can be given. What is important for such an account is what he *may* mean, and thus what he will come to mean; and this ascription can be made. Both Bloom (1973) and Greenfield *et al.* (1972) use "rich interpretation" as a means of establishing the structure underlying one-word speech by relating situational structure to the child's actions. Here this tactic is also used to relate situational structure to the intentions the child appears to be pursuing in performing those actions. For example, in discussing John and the apple (above), Greenfield *et al.* (1972: 51) note that

> Bloom would say that there is no evidence for the experience of wanting as part of the child's extralinguistic behaviour. We avoid this issue by relating *apple* to reaching and whining rather than wanting.

Here instead reaching and whining would be further related to wanting on the grounds that there does exist evidence of the child's *intentions* towards the apple: evidence provided by a knowledge of the developmental histories of these actions of reaching and whining. Thus, such intentions can be legitimately included in a description of the child's behaviour.

It does seem, then, that where certain conclusions can be drawn from a study of one-word utterances, similar possibilities are open in the case of a child who has not reached even that stage of development. And not only is it possible to describe the relationships that hold between the actions an infant performs and the situations in which he performs them by using this tactic of rich interpretation: it is also possible to delineate similar relationships between his actions and his intentions. The problem as to what medium is used for the representation of these relationships has been overcome by adopting the genetico-historical approach (see Section 5.1 on the representation of semantic force). Thus, for example, when in Observation 40 Paul points out a cup of tea, his pointing may be related to both his situational context and his intentions as shown in Fig. 5.1. Representing the values as a semantic structure of the child's actions in this manner illustrates a new theoreti-

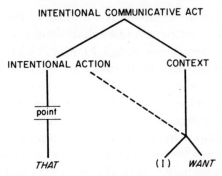

Fig. 5.1. Relationship of the action of pointing to context and intention.

cal paradigm in which to conceive of language development. The semantic forces *represented* by WANT and CUP are *implicit* in the child's actions to begin with. The child of six weeks who cries, say, eight hours after having been fed, cries not with the value of (I) WANT FOOD, but cries . . . and given the temporal context, his crying implies that he wants food. At this point Vygotsky's notion of having to possess an ability before being able to use it deliberately becomes important again. Because of the social context into which the young infant is born, he is spontaneously capable of implying certain values through his actions, and of being seen as implying them. What he is eventually able to do, as discussed in Chapter 4, is to use those actions deliberately to communicate what was previously only implicit in them. Development is thus seen as the bringing out of the implications of earlier actions.

5.3 The conjoint natural implicate

If, as is being assumed here, the world in which people live is indeterminate, then action comes to be seen as that which renders the world determinate. James (1965) notes of indeterminism that

> it admits that possibilities may be in excess of actualities, and that things not yet revealed to our knowledge may really in themselves be ambiguous. Of two alternative futures which we conceive, both may now be really possible, and the other become impossible only at the very moment when the other excludes it by becoming real itself.

A possibility only becomes real when we perform an action that brings it into the realm of what actually occurred; we thereby exclude from what actually occurred everything that did not occur. In psychological terms, performing a determinative action creates, at the same time, values (see Chapter 3) *and these values partially gain their status through those possibilities that the action negates.* This is a very simple point, but it allows an important insight to be gained on the young infant's activities.

As an example in this context, consider a child who cries. Initially this cry appears to have the status of a reaction to his existing state: it may thus be given a semantic force such as (I) *DO NOT WANT* (THAT). This reaction implies quite naturally that the child "wants" some other state of affairs: and it is upon this implication that the mother intervenes. Thus in expressing a negative attitude to some state of affairs—by making determinate through his actions the semantic force (I) *DO NOT WANT* (THAT)—the child by implication contrasts it with a possible state to which he would not express this negative attitude. Thus the performance of actions with the force (I) *DO NOT WANT* (THAT$_{(i)}$) implies the semantic force (I) *WANT* (THAT$_{(ii)}$). This implication occurs naturally and is termed here *conjoint natural implication:* (I) *WANT* (THAT) is the *conjoint natural implicate of* (I) *DO NOT WANT* (THAT)—by saying I do not want one thing I imply I do want something else.

Similarly in Observation 23 (Chapter 4) Paul cries *in reaction* to an indeterminate state, which may be termed X. By nature there must exist for him a possible alternative state, Y. Paul's crying expresses a negative attitude to state X in actuality, but by implication it expresses a potentially positive attitude to state Y. This potential positive attitude is the conjoint natural implicate of his crying. In his development he can come to make this conjoint implicate explicit. He may do so by retroactively determining what that alternative positive state is, and thus coming to use his crying not in reaction to state X but in order to attain that state Y. Again, for example, in later language development children use marked quantifiers—large, tall, heavy—before they come to use unmarked ones—short, light, etc. To say a thing is large is to imply that there are things that are not large. While at the same stages in his language development the child apparently does not realize this implication, later he does. His development could thus be conceived as one in which he realizes for himself, with the help of those around him, the conjoint natural implications of what was implicit in his own earlier abilities. The importance of conjoint natural implicates will be discussed more fully in Chapters 9 and 10.

To sum up: it is through performing actions that we are able to make distinctions in the world, to order it and make "parts" of it take on significance, to create events and objects in our perceptions: i.e. actions have values. Now any action or distinction we make possesses a conjoint natural implicate which exists necessarily—as Smedslund (1969: 8) points out:

> A crucial difference between a cause–effect relationship (A causes B) and an implication (A implies B) is that the former involves logically independent phenomena, which must be shown empirically to succeed each other, whereas the latter involves logically dependent phenomena. Physical phenomena may be linked by a theory from which it follows that A leads to B. On the other hand, a mental phenomenon A in itself implies B, without any theory.

The existence of the conjoint natural implicate of any activity does not imply, however, that the performing organism is aware of its existence: it need not in fact be aware of the semantic force of the original activity. What is important is that it is capable of coming to such awareness.

5.4 Necessary action and the structure of semantic force

Psychological indeterminism rests on the notion of choice: in a particular situation one may do either A or B or C or . . . . These *possible* courses of action exist: they lie in the field of implications opened up by that particular situation. For example, consider the possibilities open to one in expressing a request—"I would like a cup of tea, please"; "May I have a cup of tea?"; "Would you give me a cup of tea?" All these expressions of our intention are synonymous even though they are conveyed by the manipulation of differing "conceptual objects". But the argument in the case of the child insists that, firstly, he has to create these conceptual objects—he has to differentiate "you" from the actions "you" perform—and this differentiation only occurs as a result of his immersion in a social world for a relatively long period (see Chapter 9). And secondly, that the ability to manipulate these conceptual objects has a similar developmental history. In other words, these possible modes of expression, and more generally, the ability to choose a future course of action, are not initially available to the infant.

The young infant's world does not admit possible courses of action. An infant in a state of distress will cry—provided he is not "defective"—and he apparently has little option but to do this. It appears almost plausible to draw an analogy between the actions of a hungry infant and the flowing of heated metal. The possibility does not exist for metals not to glow when heated, and similarly this appears to be the case with the infant in distress: he cannot do anything but cry. It is something that occurs by *nature* and as such it has no contrasting possible alternatives.

Thus, unlike the adult, the child's behaviour is not at the outset regulated by arbitrary rules—systems of negotiated agreement—in any sphere. His behaviour is regulated by the laws of his biological structure and functioning. And so his activities do not have an arbitrary basis, nor in consequence is he capable of making a mistake. He cannot, for example, cry at the wrong time, for there are no right and wrong, correct or incorrect times. The regulation of behaviour in this way just does not admit these possibilities: it admits only one predetermined course of action, actualities which are as they are because they have to be. The import of this is that while the infant at any given moment may be in what is for him a psychologically indeterminate state—one which he cannot recognize—biologically that state is determinate. Further, since this biological state leads to *necessary actions* on the child's part, that state will not become psychologically determinate in an arbitrary way. This is because the need engendered by that state and the "object" that will satisfy it, and thus make it psychologically determinate, are fixed, in important aspects, in advance. The child's existence endows him with states that have as adjuncts certain necessary actions, and further creates for him a potential class of objects with a necessary value: "when the form is put into such a relationship with the environment, then there emerges such a thing as food" (Mead, 1934: 333; cf. Chapter 3).

However, even though the values of the child's actions are only to be found in the relationship between his existence and the world which this existence has brought into being, they are amenable to outside observers. Certain of these relations can be perceived by the mother through the necessary actions the child performs when his biology places him in one of these relations, and in acting on her perceptions the mother makes these actions effective. And as has been noted in previous chapters, it is as a result of her acting upon these perceptions, of making the child's actions effective, that she enables him to become aware of the social value of aspects of his own actions.

Linking now the notion of semantic force to that of implication and necessary natural actions, we may say that every situation engenders for the human being in it a hierarchy of implications, and at the base of each hierarchy is the emergent relationship between the child and the environment he is born into. To see what is meant here, consider again early crying. Crying is a necessary action occurring when the child is in certain biological relationships with the world. When it occurs this crying constitutes a situation, one which imputes many implications to the action—that the child is uncomfortable, that he wants something, that the mother should do something. The semantic forces of these implications that can be ascribed to the cry are: (I) (DO NOT WANT) (THAT X_1); (I) (WANT) (THAT X_2); and (YOU) (DO) (THAT X_a) respectively, where X_1 is the child's state, X_2 the object to satisfy that state, or its conjointly implicated alternative state, and X_a the action the mother must perform. These three semantic forces constitute a hierarchy in which I am proposing that (*I*) (DO NOT WANT) (THAT X_1) is the most primitive and (YOU) (DO) (THAT X_a) the most advanced and consequently the last to be determined or conceptually explicated by the child.

Crying initially possesses the semantic force (I) (DO NOT WANT) (THAT X_1): that is, the infant cries because he is in that state, and not in order to get out of it. But this cry is immediately as much part of the child's social world as of his biological one: external agents perceive it. Through the mother acting towards her child, upon her perceptions of what this crying means the infant is able to make his needs determinate, and crying quickly comes to possess the force (I) *WANT* (THAT X_2). Furthermore, when this transformation has occurred, behaviours by which he actually "approaches" an object may also have an equivalent force, i.e. be expressive of a want. Concurrently he begins to possess a structured perception of the world—he starts to see "things" with a value that derives from his natural relationship to the world. The status of his crying thus moves from that of a physiological response existing in a vacuum to an action relating him to the world he perceives, the social world in which he lives. Two examples from Piaget, which will be familiar by now, illustrate those points:

> Lucienne at 0;3(12) stops crying when she sees her mother unfastening her dress for the meal . . . Laurent between 0;3(15) and 0;4 reacts to visual signals. When I place him in his mother's arms without his touching the breast, he looks at her and immediately opens his mouth wide, cries, moves about, in short reacts in a completely significant way.
>
> (Piaget, 1952: 60)

These observations are so clear in this context that they need no expansion.

Through the infant's continual involvement in these forms of interaction, the results of the mother's responses to his actions culminate in her explicating their values for him, and in providing him with the ability to deliberately express these values in his communications with her. Eventually the child becomes able to use his actions not in response to, say, seeing something he wants, but in order to obtain that something. Later still he begins to aim his actions at this mother—he realizes for his own use the communicative function his actions previously possessed unintentionally. In accomplishing this, he brings one step nearer the possibility of explicating the conjoint natural implicate of his communicative use of actions with the force (I) *WANT* (THAT X_2), the force (YOU) (DO) (THAT X_a). In aiming his communication at his mother he exhibits an implicit knowledge of the relation between agent, action and the satisfaction of his needs. The explication of this knowledge must, however, wait on his development of symbolic communication. But, as his needs become more determinate, and he begins to communicate deliberately with his mother, he not only makes the semantic force of his actions explicit, but also their semantic intentions. There thus exists a point of contact between the position being developed here and those put forward in recent works in the philosophy of language (e.g. Strawson, 1964; Grice, 1968; Searle, 1969) and language development (e.g. Brown, 1973; Dore, 1975, 1977; Greenfield and Smith, 1976). The fact, however, that the child's actions may possess semantic intentions does not preclude them from possessing semantic force at the same time. For example, in using gestures with the semantic intention (I) *WANT THAT*, they have at the same time the *semantic force* (YOU (DO) (THAT): any semantic intention possesses one or more semantic forces as conjoint natural implicates.

There is another equally important side to this line of thought. When the child comes to use two gestures at a time (see Chapter 6) he may use one to convey a relationship, and one to convey an intended object—he communicates with a semantic force (I) *WANT THAT* X_2. This deliberate ability he possesses is structured in a way similar to that of a linguistic expression or sentence: subject-relationship-object, subject-predicate. The ability to combine gestures is prefaced by the ability to use them singly: and they are used singly with exactly the same semantic force as when in combination. The latter ability only differs from the former in that more of the semantic force is made explicit by the child. It will be argued in the following chapters that this sentence-like structuring of his early activity forms the basis of his later grammatical

speech: that grammar results from the internalization of the structure
of earlier communicative acts.

The argument so far may be outlined here in summary form as
follows:

(1) In an indeterminate world, action takes on the important property
     of being the means by which the world is made determinate. The
     performance of an action and an appreciation of its consequences
     thus create a perspective on the world for the actor.

(2) Certain actions are necessary for the child; he performs them by
     nature.

(3) By appreciating the consequences of these actions the child will
     come to a necessary perspective upon the world. The action of birth
     places the child into a certain relationship with the world, his
     necessary actions lead him to an appreciation of this relation-
     ship.

(4) His necessary actions, once he realizes their consequences, express
     this relationship: they are cast in the structural mould subject-
     relationship-object.

(5) His necessary actions possess semantic forces which in turn deter-
     mine their conjoint natural implicates, i.e. I WANT THAT
     determines within the contingencies of the child's world the seman-
     tic force YOU DO THAT by conjoint natural implication.

(6) The child's sequence of language and cognitive development could
     then be explicable by conceiving the child as an active agent
     realizing for himself through the consequences of his actions their
     conjoint natural implicates (see Chapters 9, 10 and 11).

(7) In consequence, the child's existence would determine by nature
     the form of the knowledge he may acquire, and the structure of his
     communicative abilities.

Care must be taken in delineating this position from the one
Chomsky allies himself with:

> rationalist speculation has assumed that the general form of a system of
> knowledge is fixed in advance as a disposition of the mind, and the
> function of experience is to cause this general schematic structure to be
> realised and more fully differentiated.   (Chomsky, 1965: 51–2)

Here the position being suggested is that the general form of knowledge
is fixed in advance not as a disposition of the mind, but as a consequence of existence itself. That is, out of the emergent relationship engendered between the world and the individual, and fostered through

social interaction. But given an evolutionary perspective, there seems little reason to doubt that the prior dispositions of the child will be compatible with the consequences of his existence. These prior dispositions need, however, to be conceived as the ability to realize for oneself the consequences of one's existence, and thus as only indirectly related to the form of one's knowledge. Here, then, the child's existence in the world, not simply the disposition of his mind, is seen as responsible for *the form* his emerging knowledge will take; while his biological nature is seen as responsible for *the means* by which he "develops" this know-ledge, and the society in which he lives as initially responsible for providing both *the substrate* on which his "biology" works and *the uses or ends* to which he puts his knowledge. The outline forms are thus determinate, but their contents relatively indeterminate.

An example is useful here. Consider a child who has to some extent determined his needs, and is thus on the path to making this realization-of-consequences. A simple situation in which he may become involved would be one in which he cried, was offered an object by the mother and took it, or was offered an object and refused it. Given that he has acted on the basis of some developed ability to recognize objects as relevant or irrelevant to his present state, both these actions on the child's part are totally natural tendencies. Table 5.1 tabulates these possible courses of action, and their semantic forces.

Overall the cry has the force (I) *WANT* (THAT) *NOW*. Crying makes determinate the following (I) *WANT NOW*; the termination of crying makes determinate the component (THAT). Thus the total determination of the semantic force requires two acts to be performed; an initiation and a termination of one action, crying, with or without the complementation of approach behaviour. Thus there exists func-tionally for crying a conjoint natural implicate to the semantic force (I) *WANT* (THAT) *NOW* of (I) (*DO NOT*) *WANT* (*THAT*) *NOW*, i.e. if when he is crying he is offered something that does not have the object-value characteristics capable of terminating crying and moving the interaction into the consummatory phase, the child's continued crying in the face of the offered object "exudes" the semantic force of *NOT THAT* by conjoint natural implication.

Both the establishment of crying as a gesture, having the value within the dyad of (I) *WANT*, and that of such "approach" behaviours as pointing with the force *THAT* have been discussed above. Both Darwin (1872) and Spitz (1957) have suggested that gestures (head-nodding and head-shaking) with the values *YES* and *NO* can be found

Table 5.1. Components of early crying and its termination.

Act	Context	Semantic force
(1) Crying	Any	(I) *WANT* (SOMETHING) ... (*NOW*)
(2) Termination of crying	object offered	(SOMETHING) MADE DETERMINATE AS *THAT*; THUS TOTAL FORCE AT TERMINATION: (I) (*WANT*) *THAT* ... (*NOW*)
(3) Non-termination/ continuation of crying	object offered	(I) *WANT* (SOMETHING) (*NOW*) (I) (*DO NOT*) *WANT* (*THAT*) (*NOW*) (I) *WANT* (*SOMETHING WHICH IS NOT THAT*) (*NOW*)
(4) Termination of crying + subsequent approach behaviour	object offered	(I) (*WANT*) *THAT* (*NOW*)
(5) Approach behaviour *per se*		(I) (*WANT*) *THAT* (*NOW*) (YES) (I) (WANT) *THAT* (*NOW*)
(6) Withdrawal behaviour *per se*		(I) (*DO NOT WANT*) *THAT* (*NOW*)

to originate in approach and withdrawal activities. Thus out of this interactive situation of crying there develop actions which have specific semantic forces by nature. Within the dyad it is through the "reaction" of the mother to these actions of the child that he "discovers" the meanings they implicate. The meanings implicit in the child's actions remain locked within them unless the mother creates the context in which they can be made explicit and she does so by making those actions effective. She does not *create* their values: she *draws them out* of him.

Further, these values implicate a *structure*. This structure is predetermined by his biological nature, *and so consequently is the structure of the knowledge he may gain of the relationships implicated.* What requires to be demonstrated now is that there is a direct development relationship between this early structuring of knowledge and that exhibited in his later linguistic abilities. The demonstration of this relationship is attempted in the following chapters.

6. The combination of gestures

6.1 Gestural combination

By the age of 13 (20) Paul had established the following three gestures as part of his voluntary communicative repertoire: controlled crying, making the relationship WANT determinate; pointing or vestigial reaching, making THAT object determinate; and lip-smacking. This last gesture—lip-smacking—is an action which has become removed from its original sphere of application, the acts of eating or drinking, and is used communicatively. It does not appear to be used to label objects associated with these activities—it does not identify an object in the way a word is used as a label—but rather appears to modify or clarify the relational aspects of his communications. That is, it indicates he wants an object, not to play with it, etc., but for the specific purpose of drinking or eating. Prior to the time of the following observation these three gestures had generally been employed singly—one at a time (but see Section 6.2 below).

Observation 57
Paul; age 14 (23): Mother enters the room holding a cup of tea. Paul turns from his play in her direction and obviously sees it. (i) *He cries vestigially and so attracts mother's attention; immediately he points toward her and smacks his lips concurrently.* Mother: No, you can't have this one, it's Andy's.

Mother gives me the cup of tea, and I put it on the mantelpiece to cool. Paul crawls across to me and grasps my knees. (ii) *I turn to look at him*; he looks towards the mantelpiece and *points*, turns back to me, continues to point, and *smacks his lips*.

Here at (i) Paul combines all three gestures together, and at (ii) combines two of them, in a highly efficient way, their employment taking into account the environmental contingencies of the situation in which he uses them. Had he learnt this ability in some parrot-like fashion, then it might have been expected that he would use the same strategy at (i) and (ii) in the above observation. However, in (ii) crying is unnecessary and effectively redundant since Paul already has my attention, and his behaviour illustrates that he is capable of using his gestures in harmony with his situation. It is apparent that what the child has formulated is by no means a blind, rote-like behavioural pattern, explicable perhaps by reinforcement theory from previous "fortuitous" gestural combinations (Section 6.2), but a principle which allows him to use his repertoire in a creative and situationally relevant way.

This observation shows the child using his gestures in a far more sophisticated way than has been previously noted. By combining gestures his communicative efforts gain a great deal in their functional efficiency. The whole "message" can now be made determinate by the child's actions, and does not require completion and rich interpretation by the mother: his communicative behaviour has become *context-independent*. The obvious question of importance is how this change has come about.

6.2 The co-ordination of gestures

As was noted in the discussion of Observations 38, 39 and 40 in Chapter 4, the child eventually becomes able to use his crying in a certain defined situation, that of his failure to realize an intention, in order to have that intention realized. In being able to do this, he is using his vocalization to gain assistance; it serves to summon the mother to his aid. In this type of situation then, the child attempts to attain his goal unaided, fails, or recognizes—perhaps only on isolated occasions—that he will not succeed prior to attempting direct action, and then cries to obtain assistance. In the observations noted below this mode of action is clearly illustrated.

Observation 58
Paul; age 13 (20): Paul is playing with a biro. He pokes it through the fire-guard, drops it, then tries to reach it and finds this impossible. He cries, in a very controlled fashion.
Mother looks up: What's the matter?
Paul is looking towards the fire-guard and he cries again.
Mother: Yes, the gas is roaring, isn't it?
Paul cries again and pokes his fingers through the guard.
Mother goes to pick him up.
Mother: Come on, I don't want you playing there.
He does not lift his arms in order to be lifted, but instead points towards the fire-guard. Mother follows his point visually.
Mother: Oh, there's a clever boy. Were you telling Mummy?
Thus he gets the biro back.

Observation 59
Paul; age 13 (27): Paul is playing with his football, which becomes stuck among chair legs. He tries to free it, but is unable to. He starts crying while on his hands and knees, then moves to a sitting position and continues wailing.
Mother comes in.
Mother: What's the matter? What's the matter.
Paul continues crying but also points in the direction of the chair.
Mother: Oh, have you got it stuck again? I think you do it on purpose some times,
and she gives him the ball.
Paul continues crying, but less and less vigorously, until he finally stops.

Observation 60 (See also Fig. 6.1)
Mary; age 12 (20): (1) Mary turns around in her chair and tries to pick up an apple from behind her. (2) She fails and turns back to her mother who has been watching her, and cries.
(3) Mother: What do you want?
(4) Mary gesturally reaches towards the apple.
Mother then gives it to her.

In these three observations a direct attempt to attain the goal is made in each case and this attempt is unsuccessful. Crying is used in pursuit of realizing the intention, and this use creates conditions that enable pointing to be employed. Thus the two gestures become co-ordinated to yield effective results. In the next observation Mary initially uses pointing to gain what she wants, but under inappropriate conditions so that it is unsuccessful. Her response to failing then creates a situation in which she can point successfully.

Fig. 6.1. Gesture-use at one year—see text. (Drawings from video-tape.)
1-4: Mary, age 12 (20): complex use of gestures, see Observation 60.
A-D: Mary, age 12 (20): use of object in communicative act, see Section 6.4.

Observation 61

Mary; age 10 (13): Mother has been preparing a drink for Mary. She carries the prepared drink from the stove to where Mary is seated. Mary is engaged in eating a biscuit and does not indicate any immediate interest in the drink. As mother is putting it down for her the 'phone rings. Mother puts the drink down distractedly, just beyond Mary's reach, and goes to the 'phone, out of the kitchen. Mary drops her biscuit on the floor, and leans over to look at it. She reaches towards it but it is impossible for her to pick it up. She straightens up and looks behind her to the door, and seeing no-one turns back. She sees her drink, and lazily points at it. She then waits for a moment, still looking at her beaker. Next she struggles actively to grasp the beaker but this is just impossible. She turns back to the door and then back to struggle for her drink. Again she is unsuccessful and now commences crying. The crying becomes louder and louder, moving from cries of "frustration" to screams of "rage". Mother returns and Mary's crying stops immediately. She looks at mother and lazily extends her arm in the direction of her drink.

Mother: Is that what all the fuss was about?

She gives her the beaker.

(Transcription from video-tape. No-one was present during this observation.)

The result of these gestural co-ordinations, allied to other developments occurring at the same time, such as coming to perceive occasions on which direct action will be unsuccessful prior to making any attempt, is that the child emerges with a general ability to combine his gestures "at the right time" and with respect to "the current situation". That is to say, he does not merely cry in order to create the conditions under which he can successfully point, but that he becomes able to co-ordinate *any* of his gestures as and when circumstance demands. An example of the first form of co-ordination is as follows.

Observation 62

Mary; age 11 (6): Mary is eating when she drops her spoon on to the floor. She looks down toward it but makes no attempt to reach it. She swivels round to look out of the door for her mother, and cries.

Mother: (aside, calls out) Just a minute.

Mary turns back toward her dish and looks down again toward her spoon. She turns back to the door and cries again.

Mother: O.K. I'm just coming.

Mother enters and Mary watches her intently making slight crying noises. As mother approaches she leans over the edge of her chair and points towards the ground.

Mother: (picking up spoon) No, I'll give you a clean one.

The important difference between this observation and the previous one is that Mary makes no direct attempt to obtain the spoon herself. She behaves as if she realizes she will not be able to attain her goal prior to making the attempt: she "realizes" the significance of what she is going to do *before* she does it, i.e. she cries intentionally, not in order to attract the mother's attention *per se*, but to attract it *in order that* she may get her spoon back. It appears that in the earlier cases of co-ordination the intention of using the second gesture only became possible fortuitously—the child did not cry with the intention of creating the conditions under which he could effectively use pointing, but with the intention of realizing a goal, and in so doing happened to point. Here the child is beginning to realize the effectiveness of deliberately using his gestures together, and in so doing develops the ability to make *both* a relationship and an object determinate within the same communicative episode.

Further examples of this new ability are as follows. Firstly, Observation 14, already discussed, where Peter waves his arms and points at his toy-dog, and thus his mother gives it to him. Again:

Observation 63
Peter; age 13 (14): Mother is sitting on the sofa drinking a cup of coffee. Peter crawls to her, pulls himself up by her legs, both cries and reaches towards the cup vestigially.
Mother: Oh, do you want some?
It transpires the answer was "yes".

Observation 64
Mary; age 12 (20): Mary is playing with her building blocks after finishing dinner. She has not had a thorough wash, and consequently daubs the block she is holding with sticky goo. Mother takes the block from her to wipe it. Mary produces a vestigial cry and gesturally reaches for the block (Compare this with Observation 26, Chapter 2.).

The major difference existing between the earliest gestural co-ordinations and those occurring later in the child's development can be seen most clearly on those occasions when the child has the mother's attention. In the earlier observations, 58 and 59 for example, there is a noticeable temporal separation between crying and the onset of pointing or gestural reaching: the child cries . . . and *then* points. By contrast, in the later observations, for example 63 and 64, crying and pointing occur *together*: the child cries and points *at the same time*. Similarly in Observation 57, once Paul has obtained his mother's attention he points and smacks his lips concurrently. This is again illustrated in the early portions of Fig. 6.2, Mary gesturally reaching for her beaker and crying at the same time. At the beginning of this period of co-ordination, then, the child was capable of co-ordinating two gestures, but in doing so employed them within *two* separate communicative acts. At the end of this period he can still co-ordinate two gestures but their usage is circumscribed by a single communicative act.

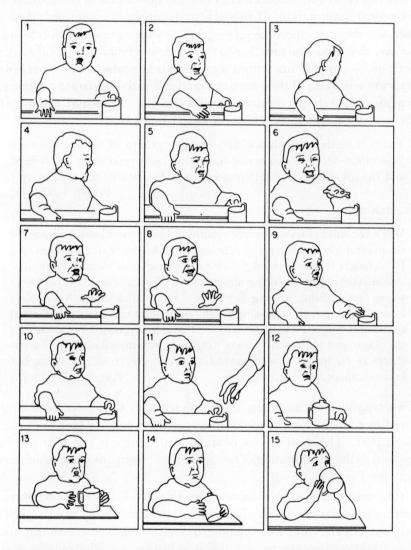

Fig. 6.2. Mary, age 12 (20): the combined use of gestures—see text. (Drawing from video-tape.) Mother is out of the room, but I am present, to the child's left. Mary reaches to the beaker in front of her and begins to cry (1-2). Note how she uses the hand furthest from the beaker and does not attempt to actually grasp it. She stops reaching and turns her head to the door, suggesting her crying is aimed at her mother (3-5). She now indicates the beaker with her other hand (6) and aims her crying at me (7-8). She gains my attention (9), and I begin to act. Mary relaxes and looks at her beaker (10) anticipating my actions, or perhaps comprehending that her request has been understood and is about to be acted upon. She thus obtains a drink (11-15).

6.3 The co-ordination and coalescence of gestures

Piaget advances within his theory of child development the concept of reciprocal assimilation. If two schemata become *co-ordinated*, that is used together in temporal sequence, there is a strong tendency for them to *coalesce*, that is to fuse together to form a new schema which subsumes both of its components within a superordinate whole. However, two separate schemata, if they are to be credited with a separate existence, organize separate perceptions around separate needs and actions. In the coalescence of such schemata Piaget notes that:

> There is neither association between two groups of images nor even association between two needs, but rather the formation of a new need and the organisation of earlier needs, as a function of this new unity.
> (Piaget, 1952: 143)

For example,

> When the child of seven or eight months old looks at unknown objects for the first time before swinging, rubbing, throwing and catching them etc., he no longer tries to look for the sake of looking (pure visual assimilation in which the object is a simple aliment for looking), nor even for the sake of seeing (generalising or recognitory visual assimilation in which the object is incorporated without adding anything to the already elaborated visual schemata), but he looks in order to act, that is to say, in order to assimilate the new object to the schemata of weighing, friction, falling, etc. There is therefore no longer only organisation inside the visual schemata but between those and all the others. (Piaget, 1952: 75–76)

Two separate schemata can thus coalesce after they have been employed in co-ordination to yield one resultant schema which embodies them both. This notion of schematic coalescence is one that can be applied to the combination of two gestures to form one communicative act (see Fig. 6.3).

One important point illustrated by Figs 6.1–6.3 is how contextual determination is effectively eliminated in the communicative strategies employed by the child. For example, by combining crying, pointing and lip-smacking together in one communicative act, the child's communicative efforts have become structurally independent of contextual determination. Functionally, however, his communication is still dependent upon the dyadic context it is employed in for its meaning. For example, while lip-smacking has a meaning which will be fairly obvious to any adult to whom it is addressed, arm-waving illustrates

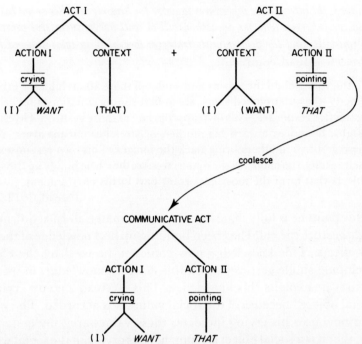

Fig. 6.3. The coalescence of two communicative schemata following their employment in co-ordination, leading to increased structure-dependence on context-independence.

how idiosyncratic these gestures of the young child really are. Their value exists within the context of the mother–child dyad and not within that of society.

Now while this context in which the child acts is one which he has created and now shares with his mother, there are certain limits to the nature of this sharing: he is not yet capable of perceiving his own actions as *equivalent* to those she performs. This accomplishment awaits a transformation in the basis of his knowledge which occurs as a result of his acquiring words. He realizes at this moment in time the values his actions have for his mother, that crying tells her that he wants, and pointing what he wants. But they only have these values for his mother because she is able to put herself in his position: he is not yet capable of putting himself in her position. For example, he can react intelligently to many of the actions his mother performs, but he still does not treat them in a "significant" way: if he points at something the mother will (usually) give it to him, but if she points at something he will not give it to her.

What he does possess, however, is *the ability to formulate his own intentions, the interpretive procedures to judge for himself whether or not his actions are successful, even whether an action will or will not be successful prior to even performing it, and the behavioural strategies to deal with the results of his own judgements.* Mead comments:

> To the young child the frowns and smiles of those about him, the attitude of body, the outstretched arms, are at first simply situations that call out instinctive responses of his own appropriate to those gestures. He cries or laughs, he moves toward his mother, or stretches out his arms. When these gestures in others bring back the images of his own responses and their results, the child has the material out of which he builds up the social objects that form the most important part of his environment.
>
> (Mead, 1912: 403)

At this point he is fully in possession of that material. In acquiring each single gesture the child has been building up his knowledge of their uses and effects. This knowledge now comes to be used by the child: in developing single gestures he establishes this knowledge, in using two gestures he exploits this knowledge. This is Mead's point: crying is a "social object" because of the social values it is accorded. The way the child now uses his crying indicates these values are "understood" by him, that it is a social object for him: he uses crying in the social world in the same way as he uses a spoon in the physical.

6.4 The implication of the object into the coalesced gestural structure

In Section 6.2 it was proposed that the result of gestural co-ordination was the emergence in the child of a "general" ability to combine his gestures "at the right time" and with respect to "the current situation". Another way of stating this is in Cicourel's (1973) terms: the child has developed fairly advanced "interpretive procedures" such that he can act with an apparent understanding of the situation he is confronted with. His actions, then, at this stage, can be tailored to suit the environmental contingencies within which they are performed. One aspect of this "tailoring" may be related to the child's later development of word usage—the substitution of an object for an object-determining gesture in a communicative act.

Figure 6.1 (A–D) shows a good example of the behaviour in question. Mary cries and holds out her beaker, her mother takes it from her and refills it; and Mary thus gets something to drink. The environmental contingencies in which Mary pursues her intention of getting a drink are such that "pointing" is unnecessary: the object can be given to the mother in the pursuit of the intention; since it is so close to the child it does not need to be pointed at. Similarly Peter's actions in Observation 22, where he brings me his squeaky ball as if in order for me to repair it, this fact is taken into account, the object is again given to the effective actor without the need for a prior object-determining gesture.

Functionally these communicative acts in which an object is involved have the same format as those incorporating an object-determining gesture, and it is in this sense that the notion of substitution has been used. Thus the child's general communicative ability may be conceived as an abstract structure into which his actions or gestures may be substituted: for example, an abstract structure such as that outlined in Fig. 6.4. The possible importance of this object-implicating form of

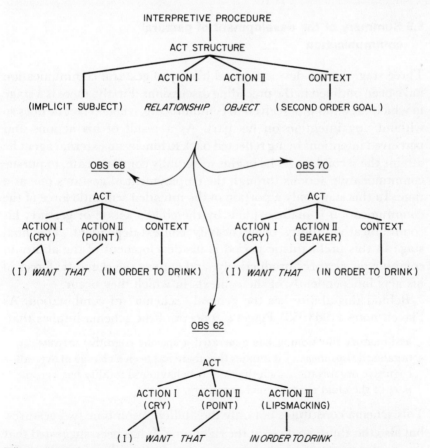

Fig. 6.4. Generalized communicative ability and its realization in three specific cases.

communicative act to the later development of word usage lies with respect to the child's coming to perceive the relationships existing between object, words and gestures. Chapters 8 and 9 put forward the idea that language develops through the interaction between the child formulating the principle that objects have names and his previously developed gestural strategies. For example, he generally points at the object he names. The action of pointing in these instances and the saying of the word both relate to the same object, that is, the gesture and the word are equivalent. It is this equivalence that allows the child to substitute a word for a gesture in a gestural strategy: instead of *pointing* at the object he wants he can *name* the object he wants. The previous implication of an object into the gestural format may have its importance in facilitating this substitution.

6.5 Summary of the development of gestural communication

Three stages in the developmental history of gestural communication have been outlined in the preceding discussions. Firstly, there is a stage in which the child is perceived to communicate, when in fact he does so without any intention on his part. As a result of his actions and perceived intentions being reflected back to him by an external agent he attains the second stage: he begins to actually communicate, to pursue communicative actions through the employment of gestures one at a time. In this stage only a portion of the intended semantic force of the communication is made explicit by the child's action or gesture, his communicative ability being heavily context-dependent. The final stage in this prelinguistic period is his development of the ability to combine his gestures productively, and convey the semantic forces of his acts independently of the contexts in which they occur.

Behind this ability lies the general "schema" of combination. As Flavell notes (1963: 53) Piaget's concept of the schema implies that

> assimilatory functioning has generated a specific cognitive *structure*, an organised *disposition* . . . it implies that there has been a change in over-all cognitive organisation such that a new behavioural totality has become part of the child's intellectual repertoire.

This schema constitutes not only the ability to combine two gestures, but also the ability to do so at the right time. It has been suggested that the development of this ability can be dealt with in terms of the

Piagetian concept of reciprocal assimilation, but there is one important difference between the use of this term by Piaget and its use here. Gestural coalescence is concerned with "schemata" that have arisen not as a result of the child's interaction with objects in the *physical* world, but as a result of his creation of objects through his transactions with the social world. His gestures do not act directly upon physical objects but through an intermediary and they take their values not from the objects they are effectively aimed at procuring, but from the actions of the intermediaries who act upon them. His knowledge has thus moved out of a totally biological sphere to encompass the social one as well. All this occurs before the appearance of language, but it will be argued that these abilities are necessary precursors for subsequent language development.

Two aspects of this argument can be usefully anticipated here. Firstly, in this "Piagetian context" there can be seen a potential parallel between Piaget's views on the relation between thought and action, and that possibly existing between language and communicative acts. Piaget maintains that the child in the sensori-motor period builds up action schemata by which he can operate on physical objects. These actions are later "internalized" so that their schematic structure becomes that by which "mental objects" are operated upon: the structures generated by action become the structures employed in thought—thought is internalized action. This suggests the parallel that language is internalized *act*: that the operations by which the child manipulates his linguistic output result from the internalization of the structures generated in his earlier communicative acts (cf. Chapter 5). The second way in which these developments are precursors of language is in their purely communicative aspect. The child develops strategies in this prelinguistic period by which he can attract and direct his mother's attention, as she does likewise with respect to him. Further they share a fairly large sphere of mutual understanding, or agreed meanings. Both these factors are of paramount importance for subsequent language use. In the latter case the potential parallel is not with Piaget's views, but with Vygotsky's: "thought and speech have different genetic roots" (1962: 41). It would appear that communication and language also have different genetic roots. The parallel with Piaget suggests a profitable approach to problems of *structure*, with Vygotsky to that of *function*. These suggestions are explored in the following chapters.

7. The emergence of words

7.1 The development of words and the problem of naming

7.1.1 The acquisition of words as "pure performatives"

The child's early learning of words presents two main problems for investigation. Firstly, how does the child come to *associate* specific sounds with specific objects. Secondly, when does he transcend these associations and come to use these sounds to *refer* to objects; for transcend these associations he must if his use of sound is to qualify as language. A framework within which to approach the first problem is implicit in the earlier descriptions of the establishment of deliberate actions from earlier spontaneous ones. Newson (1972) makes this framework explicit; he argues that

> because such happenings (i.e. events of intrinsic interest to the child) are marked and responded to by interested adults. . . they tend to become more clearly delineated as noteworthy events, so far as the child himself is concerned, in the flux of the child's ongoing activity. Thus fortuitous happenings which are socially marked come rapidly to have a rather central place in the child's consciousness. In particular happenings which are socially responded to tend firstly to be repeated more often in the future and secondly to become ritualised into familiar action patterns which have a shared social significance for the child . . . . Two examples

of shared ritualised action patterns, otherwise known as the games babies play, are: the throwing game in which a child discovers that if he throws certain objects they will first make an interesting noise and will then be picked up by his mother; the handing-things-to-people game in which the child discovers that when he holds out an object towards his mother he will induce an interesting social thank you-take-hand-back response from her. There are many similar games played by mothers and infants.

One such similar game is implicated in the child's learning to produce words. Consider, for example, the following.

Observation 65
Mary; age 11 (5): Mary is sitting in her high chair with mother next to her. She has finished eating. Some of her toys are on the table in front of her. Mother picks up a squeaky duck and shows it to Mary.
Mother: Who's this? (squeak squeak) Who is it? Is it the duck? What does the duck say?
Mary: ugh.
Mother: He doesn't say "ugh" he says "quack, quack, quack, quack" . . . "quack, quack, quack, quack". Ooh, and who's this? It's the doggie isn't it? And what does the doggie say? What does the doggie say? Mary? . . . oh, he doesn't yawn . . . What does the doggie say? "Woof, woof, woof, woof, woof", "Woof, woof, woof, woof, woof". Don't you want the doggie? Oh, you say it, "woof, woof, woof, woof, woof". Mary say it "Woof, woof, woof, woof, woof". And who's this? Who's this? It's Teddy isn't it? and Teddy says "aah". It's Teddy isn't it? Aah, love Teddy. Ah, is it Teddy? Aah.
Mary picks up the dog.
Mother: Oh, is that your doggie? What does the doggie say? What does the doggie say? What does the doggie say? "Woof, woof, woof, woof, woof". "Woof, woof, woof, woof, woof", doesn't he?

The mother's intentions for her child are pretty clear in this case. She is intent on directing the child's attention at the object in question and obtaining a specific response, or at least an acceptable approximation to it—"What does the doggie say? Mary?" . . . (Mary's attention has "wandered") . . . "Oh, he doesn't yawn" (wrong response)—"Don't you want the doggie?" (redirecting attention). "Oh, you say it" (verbal indication of her intentions).

After a few weeks of repeatedly engaging the child in similar interactions the mother can be seen to have made some progress towards this goal:

Observation 66

Mary; age 11 (28): Mother takes Mary out of her high-chair and puts her on the potty. Her toys are all in a box on the table in front of her chair.

Mother (spontaneously): Do you want Teddy?

Mary: aah

Mother: Where is he?

Mary looks around and makes to get off her potty and go to the table, but mother restrains her. Mary looks to the table and points.

Mother (going to table opposite and bringing down the box of toys): That's right, he's there, isn't he? Here he is. What does he say? What does Teddy say?

Mary: aah

Mother: Yes, he does, doesn't he?

Mary: aah

Mother pats Teddy.

Mary: aah

Mary's attention moves to the box containing her other toys, which Mother has placed on the floor near her.

Mother: Oh, what can you see in there? Doggie? (takes doggie out). Let's see who else is in here. Who's that? Is it duckie? and what does the duck say? (Mother squeaks the duck).

Mary: aah

Mother: He doesn't! What does the duck say? What does he say?

Mary: argh (reaching towards it)

Mother: Yes, I know you want it. What does he say?

Mary: woraghagh

Mother: He doesn't, he says (she squeaks it concurrently) "quack, quack, quack", doesn't he? "quack, quack, quack".

Mary: gh, gh

Mother: Yes, he does.

Mary (looking at Teddy): aah

Mother: And that's aah is it, that's aah Teddy.

Mary: aah

Mother: And who's this, what does he say? What does doggie say? What does doggie say?

(No response from Mary. Mother squeaks duck).

Mary: gah

Mother: quack!

Mary: gah

Mother: Ooh, aren't you clever.

In this latter example Mary gives evidence that she is beginning to relate specific sounds with specific objects. This relating of sound and object is used in a game in which she gains equivalent rewards to those she acquires in other social games at this time: "praise", or what Newson (1972) termed "an interesting social thank you . . ." Such a social game is as follows:

Observation 67
Mary; age 11 (14): Mother is at the sink, preparing vegetables for cooking. Mary is acting as a shuttle-service between the vegetable-rack and mother. Typically their interactivity is as follows:
Mary takes a green bean from the vegetable rack, carries it to mother, holds it out. Mother takes the bean:
"Thank you" (and smiles). Mary returns to the vegetable rack and brings a carrot, offers it to Mother. Mother takes it, smiles: "There's a good girl, thank you" and so on.

The game Mary is playing here is a means and end in itself, played because it gains "an interesting social thank you-take-hand-back response". It does not appear to extend beyond this: just because her actions are congruent within their greater frame of reference does not mean that she is helping mother prepare dinner. This conjunction is probably fortuitous: she will dole out vegetables to any visitor in any context so long as they continue to "play the game".

Early "word play" appears to be of a similar character; but further, it also has the characteristics of the activities described during Mary's learning to feed herself. A specific activity is required on the child's part to gain the desired response, and the criteria which this activity has to satisfy become more and more rigorous as the game progresses. The closer the child's vocalization comes to satisfying those criteria, the better the response provided by the mother.

Such games are probably erected out of spontaneous, yet fortuitous, acts of vocalization, by the child, these acts being seized upon by the adult and created as significant. Greenfield (1973) describes one such strategy for creating a vocalization as significant as follows:

Lauren, a girl, produced "Dada" for her first word. We (her mother and father) started helping her to understand what these syllables meant at the point when they began to appear frequently as a spontaneous sound pattern. This point of spontaneous articulation was also identified by F. H. Allport (1924) as a first step in the development of language proper and a necessary preliminary to imitating the speech sounds of others.

In Stage I (Lauren was eight and one-half months old) we successfully encouraged her to imitate the sound at will. Basically, we started by imitating *her*. This procedure seemed to provoke her to repeat her original sound. We would, of course, act pleased when she did this, but it seems that the important factor was learning that if *she* said a sound, *we* would say it. Indeed, Piaget (1962) has described this same phenomenon in great detail.

A similar situation exists in Observations 65 and 66. Sounds that Mary has previously produced spontaneously are now the focus for a game: the mother attempts to get Mary to produce these sounds at a specific instant.

At this stage the sound or "word" produced by the child constitutes a "pure performative" in the sense developed by Austin: "it indicates that issuing of the utterance is the performing of an action—it is not normally thought of as just saying something" (1962: 6–7). In the sense with which it is being used here, the pure performative differs from Austin's conception in that it could *never* be thought of as "just saying something", since the child is incapable of saying anything: it is just an "empty sound" from the referential perspective. It does, however, become an utterance with a consistent production associated with some object, and it is "performed" in a clearly delineated situation each time.

The majority of very early "word" learning probably occurs in this manner; a sound is established as consistently reproducible *before* it acquires any meaning beyond its performance in the ritualized game situation. The next step is for it to acquire a referential meaning, and then to be finally exploited for a communicative purpose. Before discussing these processes, however, a case that appears to exist beyond these confines will be described.

The case in question is the further development of frustrated crying. The description to be given here is congruent with what occurred in all three children in this study, two other children who were briefly observed at this stage in their development, and possibly also in those observed by Greenfield and Smith (1976) (see below). In combination with pointing, frustrated crying functions both to attract attention and indicate that the child wants something. Its use in this way is voluntary; consequently it lacks many of the properties of true crying, having become highly vestigial. Its production is very nasal and naturally tends to be comprised of a nasal consonantal commencement, followed by a long nasal vowel: "ma". The apparent "emphatic" usage of this cry was not in these cases obtained by increasing the volume of its production alone, but by repetition: "ma, ma, ma". This intense repetition tends to mutate the "m" towards an "n", but this change is of relative unimportance to the mother's perception of the sound.

As must be obvious by now, the mother interprets such crying as the word "mama", and she produces the requisite social marking in her reactions eventually to establish the cry as an intentionally produced "mama". In fact, as will be noted below, this "word" appeared to have no reference to the mother, but was used with its initial value of *WANT* or of attracting attention. It becomes directly established with a functional reference, as opposed to most words, which first exist as pure performatives and then acquire objective reference, both these stages existing in a communicative vacuum before acquiring any functional reference. In this case the sequence is reversed, the child learns the function of the word prior to learning or discovering its inherent reference to a significant object in his environment, his mother.

7.1.2 From association to naming

The learning of words presents two problems: the first concerns the establishment by the child of sound–object associations, and this process has been described immediately above. The second problem is the more difficult one to tackle; when does the child pass beyond simple association and come to use sounds to name objects? The major difficulties presented by this problem are conceptual: what are the characteristics of the act of naming, and what criteria are there that can be used to judge the status of some noise the child makes? That these conceptual problems are the important ones can best be brought out by describing the course of events that lead to the child apparently being able to actually name objects, and then reflecting upon that course of events.

To begin, it is best to return to Observations 65 and 66, which have previously been used to illustrate the development of words as "pure performatives". The game is so structured that not only does Mary have to produce the correct sound to gain her social reward, she also has to produce it at the correct time. That time is marked within the game by the mother, usually in two ways: firstly she prefaces the point at which a response is expected with a question, an utterance having a specific intonation pattern; and secondly she indicates the "object to be named" in some way.

What the child has to come to do at this point in time is produce a noise. In its global aspects every game is the same, but it is *internally*

E

differentiated: a different sound must be produced for a different object. This internal differentiation is of great importance since it makes a *difference* apparent to the child in what are otherwise two identical games. Further, the "object to be named" is the only constant in the game, the rules of which the mother is continually changing in attempting to "shape" the child's vocalizations. These factors perhaps combine to make the "object to be named" stand out in the child's perception. For example, the rituals of "Who's this? Is it Teddy? What does Teddy say?" and "Who's this? Is it the duck? What does the duck say?" differ only in the object offered, and one word uttered. When the stage is reached at which the child correctly performs a differential response, she is beginning to use the sound with respect to the correct significant "event": she responds to the correct significant differences in two similar social rituals. In this way "gh" and duck become associated, as do "aah" and Teddy. Similar results occur when the ritual is built around a picture book. It seems that what mothers do quite naturally is to structure ongoing language games firstly to match the level of the child's ability, and secondly in such a way that the child has little option but to make the correct significant object–word association.

Next, in much the same way as was noted in the earlier development of gestures, the time at which the child's behaviour occurs in the interaction begins to change. Rather than waiting until the mother initiates the game by showing some object to the child and waiting for a sound to be produced, the child starts to single out the object himself and produce his sound. Essentially the initiation of the "game" passes from the mother to the child, so that rather than the mother directing the child's attention to some object and him responding, he directs his mother's attention to the object, and then "responds" as well. Mary in Observation 66 seems to say "aah" in response to the word "Teddy", and then points out where Teddy is. This "coming to use sounds as if they were 'words' which 'referred' to objects" can be described as a three stage process. These three stages may be illustrated using Peter as an example. Firstly, there is a period of teaching in which the mother always initiates the interaction, showing some object to the child and demanding some particular response. During this period Peter becomes more proficient in his responding. This period has the same characteristics as that described above for Mary, Observations 65 and 66.

Secondly, a period seemingly transitional between the first and the third in which initiation of the interactions passes to the child, such that he "names" an object which he singles out during the "game" and "names" it without being asked to; for example:

Observation 68
Peter; age 13 (13): Peter is playing on the floor with mother. I am sitting against the sofa.
Mother (to me): This is his favourite book. Where's the moo-cows, Peter? Where's the moo-cows? Hey? You show Andy your book. (Gives the book to Peter.)
Andy: Come on over here then.
Peter comes and gives the book, placing it in my outstretched hand.
Mother: What's that, hey?
Andy: Well . . . what is it?
Mother: Is that a moo-cow?
Andy: And what's that? (pointing at lamb)
Mother: He's waiting for you to say it first.
Andy: Oh, I've got to go first have I?
Mother: Yes.
Andy (pointing): What's that then, is it a baa-lamb?
Peter: (laughs)
Andy (pointing): And is that a moo-cow?
Peter: (laughs again)
Mother (points): And what's this one here . . . doggie?
Peter: Doh dug
Mother (points): Yes, that's it, and what's this one?
Peter: Do-ug
Andy: No, that's a moo-cow, silly.
Peter (laughs and pushes hand over book): Dee dah.
Mother: No, that's not a gee-gee, that's on another page.
She turns to that page.
Andy (pointing): There he is, there's the gee-gee. That's a gee-gee.
Peter: Dee. Dee dah.
Mother: That's it. (points) What's this?
Peter: Dah.
Mother: Yes, doggies.
Peter (pointing): Dah.
Mother: No, that's a cat.
Peter (pointing to a third animal): Dooee.
Mother: No, that's not a boo (cow), he's on another page.
Andy (turning page): There he is, look!
Peter: Ma boo.
Andy: That's right.
Peter (pointing to animal): Gee-eh.

Mother: No, gee-gees on another page.
Peter (pointing to another animal): Gee-eh.
Mother: That's a baa lamb. (to me) It's very confusing, he just says the one
          word most of the time. (To Peter) That's a baa-lamb, it goes baaaa.

During this period, those cases in which the child has acted as initiator almost invariably occur within a game situation. However, towards the latter end of the period isolated cases occur outside such a context, for example:

Observation 69
Peter; age 13 (13): (a) Mother is putting Peter's slippers on.
Peter reaches upwards, laughs and shrieks "Lieee".
Mother: Yes, its the light.
Peter: Dieee.
Mother: That's right, light, light.
(b) I am talking to Mother. Peter comes up to me and touches my wrist.
Peter: Dik do.
Andy: Yes, its a tick tock.
I continue talking to mother, the above occurring without intruding into our conversation.

Concurrent with these developments the child is being taught new words in "game" situations, and thus expanding his vocabulary (he expands it to his mother's satisfaction, in Peter's case I could seldom tell one "word" from another with any certainty). His ability to associate a word and an object is further enhanced by his becoming able to respond to a variant initiative question of the mother's: not "what's this, is it a moo-cow?" but "where is the moo-cow?" An early form of this has already been noted in Observation 66 where Mary is asked "Where's Teddy?" and she attempts to fetch Teddy but after restraint points at him. In Peter's case the following observation illustrates a similar instance at a later stage of development—the ability to look for objects:

Observation 70
Peter; age 13 (14)
Mother (to me): He's (Peter) a proper comedian. You put a cushion on the
          floor and he lays down and goes to sleep, or at least he pretends to.
She then gets Peter to demonstrate this.
Mother: Hey, Peter, wake up, where's Bugs Bunny? Where is he? Go and get
          him.

Peter gets up and walks to the door (his bedroom is just off the living-room, and Bugs Bunny is in there).
Mother: Yes, he's through there, go and get him.
Peter leaves the room and goes into his bedroom.
Mother: Are you getting him?
Peter re-emerges dragging a huge inflatable pink rabbit.
Mother: That's a good boy.
Peter (drops rabbit and points at the television): Kee.
Mother: Yes, that's the television, and that's Bugs Bunny.
Peter grasps Bugs Bunny again.
Mother: Ah, love that Bugs Bunny.
Peter drops Bugs Bunny and walks out of the room.
Mother (calling after him): What are you after now? Where's that nice football?
Peter appears as she is speaking with the football and drops it: Dair-gair.
Andy: Yes, football.
Mother (laughs): Sounds like tick-tock, doesn't it?
Peter (pointing): gair.
Mother: Yes, that's the television.

This observation is interesting in more ways than just the one it is being used for here: it shows Peter performing symbolic play, which must bear a close relationship to true language use; how close an understanding mother has of Peter by now, that she can effectively anticipate his fetching the football; it perhaps sheds light on Observations 16 and 17 where Peter apparently progresses to ask for objects to be brought to him; and thus it also may shed some light on the development of later significant communication (see Section 9.2). These aspects will not be pursued further here, as the prime importance of this observation is the way it illustrates the developing bond in the child's conception of object and word. Peter's conception of the words "Bugs Bunny" is apparently one in which they *refer* to the object, and are not merely associated with it. It seems an almost inescapable conclusion that Peter can at last be said to label objects—to refer to them by their names:

Observation 71
Peter; age 13 (13): Peter is kneeling on the sofa looking out of the window. I am next to him. Mother is sitting apart from us in the room. Peter turns to me and looks at my watch. He grasps it and laughs.
Peter: Di.
Mother: Di . . . dis and dat. (Laughs)

Andy: It's a tick-tock.
Peter: Ay dok.
Andy: Yeh, that's right.
A car drives past and the noise attracts Peter's attention.
Peter: Gar! Gar. Gar.
He continues watching until it is out of sight.
Peter (pointing): Liee, Liee.
Andy: You what?
Peter: Liee, Liee, Dere, Dere.
Mother: It's the telegraph poles or street lights, he gets them confused.
At mother's voice Peter turns from the window towards her.
He points at the ceiling.
Peter: Liee.
Mother: Yes, light.
Peter (pointing at TV): Gair.
Mother: Television.
Another car goes past, Peter turns to the window.
Peter (pointing): Gar, Gar.
He watches until it disappears. I direct his attention to a seagull.
Andy (pointing): What's that?
Peter (pointing): Ka-Ka.
Andy: It's a seagull.
Peter: Ka-Ka.
Mother: He calls birds "Ka-Ka" after all the crows.
Peter: Ka-Ka (points at a dog which has appeared). Darg.
Mother: Is it a doggie?
Peter turns to mother and falls off the settee.

This observation illustrates the third stage in the process—he initiates the singling out of the object and he also gives the "correct" noise without prompting. (It will be noticed that the observations used to illustrate this developmental process do not occur in a linear sequence but are all drawn from Peter's behaviour at the same age. I am most grateful to Roger Clark (1978) for pointing out to me that such a sequence actually exists.)

The *impression* that arises from looking at these developments in the child's use of his "words" *suggests* that there has occurred a change in his knowledge, such that it now admits an understanding that objects have names. It is difficult to go beyond using notions such as "impression" and "suggestion", for hard evidence that the child attains to the principle that objects have names is difficult to find. Jesperson (1922: 114) notes that

What Stern tells about his own boy is certainly exceptional, perhaps unique. The boy ran to a door and said, "das?"—(That?—his way of asking the name of a thing). They told him "tur". He then went to two other doors in the room, and each time the performance was repeated. He then did the same with the seven chairs in the room . . .

Were all children to behave like this it would undoubtedly ease the task of the psychologist.

Definitive evidence that the young infant has made such a transition—that they name, refer to or can stand for, an object—is much less clear cut than this. Firstly there is the fact that a child will often use an invented word for an object he does not know the name of. The obvious implication is that he must know in some way that objects can have names for him to invent one. Moore (1896: 125) notes this occurrence in an older infant:

> with the entrance into the eighty-second week (19 months) the child began to give a name to each object with which he came in contact. If he did not know or recall the name given to it by others he invented a name.

In Peter's case he was apparently doing this much earlier, for example Observation 13 where he points at objects in the "game-playing" situation and exclaims "*dair*" if he does not know the object's name. Similarly in Observation 72 where he is confronted with two unfamiliar objects:

Observation 72
Peter; age 13 (13)
Peter (pointing at television): Dair.
Mother: Television, it's a bit of a long word to get your tongue round, isn't it?
Peter (pointing at microphone): Dair! Dair!
Mother: What's that? . . . . That's a microphone, another big word.
Peter (crawls to microphone, picks it up and pulls at it): Dair, dair (he looks along its cable and points at the tape-recorder). Dair! Dair!
Mother: That's Andy's tape-recorder.

In both these cases Peter's "word" could equally well be a means of directing his mother's attention, or be part of a larger social ritual.

Secondly, there is the well-documented phenomenon of the extension of the reference of a word that the child possesses; for example, Peter's use of *lieee* in Observation 71. Generally, interest has been focused on such extensions with respect to the way in which the child builds up a concept of certain classes of objects, and in the case of *lieee* the progression from ceiling-light to street-light to telegraph pole would be the matter under attention. But here its major importance is its implication with respect to the child's knowing that objects have names. Through possessing the word *lieee* he is able to perceive similarities between disparate objects—only because he possesses some understanding of the relationship between his word and those objects.

Thirdly, words now begin to be acquired in a different way: the laborious game of building up an association between a sound and an object recedes, and the child increases his vocabulary in some other, and as yet barely understood, way. This again implies that the basis of his ability is more than being able to associate a particular sound with a particular object, but that he has "gone beyond the information given" towards knowing some principle, and is thus provided with a guide for his later learning. And fourthly, the way in which the child extends the uses to which his words may be put similarly suggests his possession of the principle that objects have, or can have, names (see below, Section 8.4 and Chapter 9). Yet as has been noted, none of this evidence can be taken as conclusive. But if it is accepted that on the basis of finite experience the child *has* come to possess some general principle, then it has to be admitted that he has not learnt this principle, but has *created* it for himself out of that finite experience. Whilst it has been the mother's intention that her child should learn that objects have names, and what these names are in specific cases, she is in fact incapable of teaching him this. All that the mother can do is to teach the child to associate a specific sound with a specific object; and all that the child can *learn* are those specific associations. It has to be left to the child to discover creatively the principle of naming that is inherent in what he has been taught. The mother provides the child with "data" in such a way that given his spontaneous abilities it is perhaps inevitable he comes up with the right answer.

7.2 The structure of naming

Given that the child *can* name objects, what might the structure of this ability be? Greenfield *et al.* (1972) suggest on the basis of their data the structure "That is X":

> In two . . . cases of pointing messages, a name was instigated by the question "What is that?" The word may therefore be considered to fit into the structural framework provided by the question. Thus, it implies the

structure "That is X". Since, in each case [the child] also is pointing to the thing he names, the question provides evidence that pointing is the gestural equivalent of the demonstrative "that", which locates the thing to be named.

Naming is almost invariably associated with pointing (cf. Greenfield and Smith, 1976: 84–91) and as has been seen, pointing is established well before the emergence of this new ability as a means of object determination, having a semantic force *THAT*. Thus it is reasonable to structure naming as shown in Fig. 7.1. If this structure is compared to those typically used in the child's communication prior to the appearance of words, for example, Fig. 7.2, it can immediately be seen that there exists a crucially important structural difference in the semantic forces of these two activities. For the first time, the child is not reflexively implicated in the structure of the force of his act: the value the object is endowed with is independent of his own actions. This difference exists because the ability constituted by naming is established in a different way to these earlier productive abilities. There are four main differences in these two abilities.

Firstly, the structure of naming is almost propositional. For the first time an action on the part of the child is capable of being judged true or false; the semantic force of his actions being open to determination by

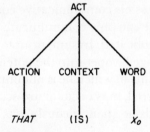

Fig. 7.1. Structure of acts of object-naming.

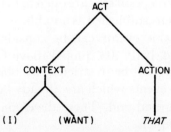

Fig. 7.2. Example of gestural structure, specifically pointing.

arbitrary social agreement, and not by non-arbitrary biological states. Secondly, such near-propositional relationships, which by nature do not implicate the child in their structure, provide the basis for the development of objective knowledge. Prior to this point the child has learnt the value of an object in terms of the relationship it has to himself through the mediation of his actions upon it. From this point onward there exists the possibility of his giving values to objects which stem from their relationships with other objects; relational systems having an existence independent of his own: he opens up World 3 for himself.

Thirdly, he is using language proper for the first time, but he is not using it communicatively. Granted he can now "state facts", but in an interpersonal context this ability can only be of value in that it brings a great deal of social reward. He has established language, but he is not yet putting it to communicative ends.

Fourthly, because of the possibilities of placing objects in relationships in which he is not reflexively implicated and of the conjoint fact that he now has the possibility of making statements that are free of any immediate value, a subtle change in the time structuring of the reference of his utterances is opened up. Prior to language his communicative ability is focused totally on the immediate future; *its only concern is with the pursuit and furthering of his own intentions.* He *cannot* communicatively comment on events that *have* happened, he can only react to them: he can only address his communicative comments to events that *will* happen. Likewise he can only communicate about events in which he himself as agent is implicated. In sum, prior to language, he is totally egocentric. With language he opens up the potential ability not only to communicate about events in which he is not implicated but also about events which have occurred, may occur or are occurring. In discovering these properties of words he spontaneously acts to erect them as symbols.

Finally, it may be noted that objects are not the only significant aspects of the child's perception that are open to being labelled. Certain events have already been established as notable or socially marked; and in Mead's terms, notable events can be considered as constituting *"social objects"* (cf. Mead, 1912: 403, quoted above, Chapter 6). Thus his ability to name need not be restricted to objects, but may include those important events which are already "objectified" for him as having a beginning and end. These developments are discussed further in the next chapter.

8. The early use of words

8.1 The development of word usage

8.1.1 Introduction

From this point onward the discussion is based largely on the work and data of Greenfield and her collaborators. Two reports of this work have appeared: a working draft by Greenfield *et al.* (1972) which gave rise to the published study of Greenfield and Smith (1976). Any study necessarily undergoes revision between its early and published forms. By and large I draw upon the more readily available 1976 version, but on occasions I find it useful to resort to the earlier manuscript. Where this is done without qualification it reflects the fact that there is no substantive change between the earlier and later views of the authors. But where the 1972 version is used in preference to that of 1976 and a substantive point is at issue, the reasons for doing so are noted.

Greenfield's study followed

> two children (Matthew and Nicky) . . . from the emergence of their first meaningful words through the one-word stage to the establishment of word combinations. The data reported . . . end at a point where single-word utterances were in the minority for the first time.   (1976: 31)

In their own words,

> the plan of the study was to combine diary observations of infrequent and

critical events with formal observation sessions. The two sources of data were seen as complementary. At the beginning of language development. children speak very infrequently. On the one hand, a scheduled observation session, even one lasting an entire day, might yield little or no speech; on the other hand, one does not want to miss any data in this crucial early period.   (1972: 61)

The diaries cover the period from 8 (19) (eight months, nineteen days) to 21 (8) in the case of one child, and 7 (22) to 22 (0) in the case of the other child; formal observation sessions being from 18 (4) to 24 (23), and 12 (15) to 22 (1) respectively, conducted at roughly monthly intervals. The study provides a complete corpus of each child's utterances as appendices, and each utterance is accompanied by a description of the context within which it occurred.

Might there be any relationship between the child's previously developed gestural abilities and his newly emerging language abilities? Initially, these early language behaviours—the naming of objects and certain actions—do not possess an inherent communicative function. At this time the child has established the beginnings of language, but he has not discovered a communicative use for it. It would seem intuitively plausible that rather than his "starting from scratch" and developing such a communicative ability *de novo*, he will fall back on that which has arisen through his earlier use of gestures: that in some way there will be an interaction between the older gestural system and that of his newly emerging language. For example, the child's communicative system of gestures at the time he develops the ability to name objects contains strategies that have been given the structure shown in Fig. 8.1. With the advent of the naming function he also possesses the ability shown in Fig. 8.2. Thus, it is easy to see how, *in theory*, the action of pointing at an object as part of a communicative act, making THAT determinate, could instead be equivalently performed by the use of a word; for in the naming structure, pointing and the naming word both refer to the same object, thus making them functionally equivalent. It is further possible to see how, in a similar way to the earlier coalescence of single gestural acts to yield multi-gestural acts, these two structures could coalesce, yielding productive behaviour having the structure given in Fig. 8.3. That is, the word could be used in the pursuit of an intention. Alternatively, the opposite but complementary development may also be expected to occur; crying could be replaced by a word, and then used in combination with pointing (see Fig. 8.4).

Similarly, on the basis of these theoretical considerations, it might

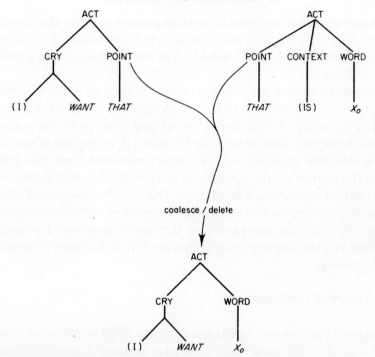

Fig. 8.1 (top left). Gestural communication immediately prior to words.
Fig. 8.2 (top right). Naming ability.
Fig. 8.3. (bottom). Possible use of words in pursuit of intentions.

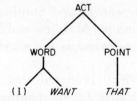

Fig. 8.4. Alternative possibility for demands with words.

further be expected that *both* gestures could be substituted by words, and thus the infant would be capable of making two-word utterances almost immediately. It is quite obvious that this expectation is not realized in the child's development: children invariably use single words prior to using two-words, and there is quite a considerable gap between these two periods of word usage, anything between four months and one year (cf. Leopold, 1939:2). But the fact that this expectation is not realized does not mean that the notion of word–gesture substitution/coalescence is vitiated. Substitution does seem to occur and arguably occupies a most important point in the development of language, but for various reasons to be discussed this substitution does not occur in what would seem the obvious and straightforward fashion.

While this notion of word–gesture substitution is an important one, it is not the only one that has to be considered. The other major point is the way in which the previously developed concept of the conjoint natural implicate can shed light on the child's development of new uses for his language capacities. This chapter examines these two points within the context of: the apparently unique developmental history of early volition utterances; a further discussion of the structure of object- and action-naming and its relation to the problem of "objectification"; and finally with the emergence of the use of language for making demands or pursuing intentions. Chapter 9 then discusses subsequent developments.

8.1.2 Volitional utterances

As I stressed previously, words learnt by the child as names of objects are not used in the same communicative manner as gestures: words function more as indicatives than imperatives. This creates the problem of how they eventually come to be used in that way. But not all words are acquired as names in the first place. One class of utterance, termed "volitional" by Greenfield and Smith (1976), is used communicatively from the beginning. Matthew and Nicky had three main words for expressing volition—*mama, no* and *yes*. Here I will concentrate solely on the word *mama*.

Greenfield and Smith (1976: 91) conclude that "volitional utterances appear only after the indicative i.e. the naming of objects is established". There are reasons, however, to doubt this point; they are outlined below. Examples of Matthew's use of the word *mama* during Observation session 1 are shown in Table 8.1 Greenfield *et al.* discuss *mama* as follows:

> *Mama* becomes the first general request that the children use. Its identity to the word for mother is not significant, since Piaget (1923) cites an example of a child using his grandfather's name in this way. In this usage the child says *mama* or some variant in a whine while reaching for some object. In the case of Nicky, this use of *mama*, beginning at 13 (19), does not refer to his mother: Nicky usually called his mother by name rather than *mama* but used *mama* even for requests to his father, although he

Table 8.1. Uses of *Mama* at Matthew I—12 (15) and 12 (22).

Preceding context	Modality	Event	
	M pointing to whining *ma*	microphone	
	M reaching for whining, repeats *mama*	orange juice glass	
	M looking at whining *mama*	bottle of milk	
Mother holding doll.	walks to whining *mama*	doll	
	N reaching toward whining, repeats *mama*	tape recorder	
With mother in room, sitting on rocking chair that he has stopped rocking.	M whining, repeats *mama*		(to be taken off)
	N holding whining *mama*	rocking horse	(to ride)
	N pointing to whining *mama*	bell button	(to push)

Note: Situational descriptions in parentheses relate to later events which confirm the semantic interpretation. Broken horizontal rules separate utterances that were not part of connected discourse.
(From P. M. Greenfield and J. Smith, *The Structure of Communication in Early Language Development* Reprinted by permission.)

already had the word *dada* in his vocabulary (1972: 92–3). In the most interesting example, Nicky said *daddy mommy daddy*, 19 (19), when he wanted his father to pick him up. In this sequence, *daddy* appears to be the term of address, *mommy* the demand element. *Mama* as a request pivot ultimately drops out. Therefore, it seems best to think of *mama* and its variants as initially retaining an expressive quality characteristic of pre-linguistical verbal communications, a kind of performative with an object. Looking at *mama* from the perspective of later development, it is the first instance of the Demand modality.   (1976: 92)

Earlier, in Section 7.1.1, the development of *mama* from gestural, "frustrated", crying was noted. In its later usage, frustrated crying was used in conjunction with pointing to yield the coalesced act-structure already given (as in Fig. 8.5). This structure is directly applicable to the use of *mama* reported by Greenfield *et al.* (1972; 1976), with the difference that ACTION 1 has been established at the level of a word, i.e. for Matthew I, usage 2, Table 8.1. Thus we have the structure given in Fig. 8.6. This structure will deal with most of these utterances, and for this purpose the generalized structure shown in Fig. 8.7 may be given.

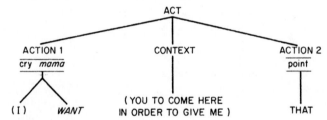

Fig. 8.5. Use of vocative in communicative acts.

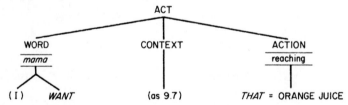

Fig. 8.6. Matthew 1, Utterance 2.

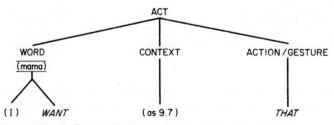

Fig. 8.7. General structure for vocative use.

Mama, then, has functional and not objective reference, and an equivalent status to the action-as-gesture it replaces. Thus, the notion of word–gesture substitution is not applicable here. The child does not learn the word *mama* beyond his use of gestures, as he does with object names. Rather, *mama* is a direct transformation of the gestural form: not an entity that has been *substituted for* a gesture, but one which has *developed out of* a gesture. In this sense, *mama* is not truly the "first instance of the Demand modality", for that instance has a longer history. When *mama* qualifies as a true word is perhaps impossible to judge with any exactness. The status of *mama* as an utterance is thus problematic, and this sets it apart from the rest of early language development.

On a more positive note, however, the proposed structure of communicative acts involving *mama* is further substantiated by looking forward to future developments as well as back to previous ones. Following the establishment of this function, and those of Object of Demand, and Action in a Demand Context (see later this chapter), *mama* becomes a component in the first two-word sequences produced by both Matthew and Nicky, i.e. mama plus a second member which is the name of a wanted Action or object. There is a transition roughly given in Fig. 8.8, but for a fuller discussion see Section 10.1.

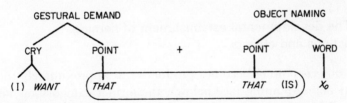

Fig. 8.8. Juxtaposition of gestural demand strategy and object-naming structure.

8.1.3 Objectification

Objectification is a two-fold process. It refers firstly to the development of knowledge by the child whereby he knows of objects independent of his own subjective interactions with them. That is, he develops knowledge of *the relationships existing between one object and another,* where the relationships are directly socially verifiable, for example, the relationship "A is larger than B" is objective, socially agreed and easily verified. Secondly, it is concerned with the creation in the child's perceptions of the very objects whose interrelations he comes to know. This second point is the core of the well-aired Sapir-Whorf hypothesis: that the essence of socialization is coming to agree with one's society on how to cut nature up into "chunks". For example, "the cup is green" is an objective statement, and green is an objective quality. But it is only an objective quality through social convention: the continuous changes in the visible spectrum are created as discontinuous cultural objects. And as we know, different cultures draw their lines in different ways. Similarly, the child is faced with the problem of discovering what the objects are in his culture. Not only is he faced with the problem of concept attainment in the familiar sense of physical objects, but also in the case of objectified "events" such as actions and states. For example, in Table 8.3, what does Nicky's word *down* refer to? The experience of going down, the resultant change in state, the resultant change in position, etc? *Down* itself has to be created with objective reference. The point to be emphasized here is that words are not acquired as mere labels for pre-existing concepts; rather that a word new to the child's vocabulary brings with it a distinction new to his perception. Thus the developments during the appearance of verbal communication illustrate not only the development of language, but also that of objective knowledge. This view is discussed further in the next chapter.

8.1.4 The developmental establishment of naming: actions and objects

While object-naming becomes productive at approximately the same time as action-naming (see below), the former category, as noted in Section 7.2, is important in that structurally the child is not implicated in what he is making determinate. By contrast, action-labelling does not appear to have this structure. In Greenfield and Smith's opinion (1976: 112), action-labelling words grow out of pure performatives, and "differ from the earliest Performatives . . . in that there is a much more clear-cut and language-like separation of word and act: the Action word *refers* to the act rather than being *part* of it". But even given this referential aspect, action-labelling has a different nature of object labelling *because "the referent" is the child's own action.* Perhaps because of their developmental relation to pure performatives, the early action words of the child function to label only *his* actions (see Table 8.2).

Table 8.2. Different uses of *down* to express action or state of agent at Nicky II—18 (27).

Preceding context	Modality	Event
	N sits down *down*	
	N sits down *down*	
	N sits down *down*	
	N sitting down *down*	
	N gets down *down*	
Where are you going?	N gets down from *down*	chair
	N gets down from *down*	chair
	N getting down from *down*	table
	N getting down from *down*	table
	N has gotten down from *down*	table
	N steps across to *down*	sofa
	N trying to get up on *down*	sofa
	N trying to get up on *down*	table
	N has just gotten up on *down*	table

Table 8.2. (cont.)

Preceding context	Modality	Event
	N gets up	
	down	
	N gets up	
	down	
	N gets up	
	down	
	N standing up	
	up	

Note: Broken horizontal rules separate utterances that were not part of connected discourse. (From P. M. Greenfield and J. Smith, *The Structure of Communication in Early Language Development.* Reprinted by permission.)

Further, he only labels them when he is performing them—unlike objects which have a stable existence in time, an action only exists while it is being performed. It thus seems more appropriate to conceive of the structure of this ability in terms of (I) (AM DOING) X_a rather than (THAT) (IS) X_a. That is, the child is not yet able to make an objective distinction between an agent and the actions he performs. To be able to do this, developments must occur in his linguistic abilities as they relate to objects, i.e. utterances in which he is not implicated. As Greenfield and Smith point out, "naming is the basis for subsequent language use" (1976: 91). With the advent of naming, the child opens up the possibility of knowing about objects *as objects* at the symbolic conceptual level: he opens up for exploitation an objective world in which knowledge rests in the relationship one conceptual object or objectified event bears to another.

Because it is so necessary to keep in mind the future developments of an ability at any particular instance, it is not profitable to leave the semantic force of action-labelling as it is at present. Certainly the form that has just been advanced is adequate to indicate that action-naming is not yet propositional. But it is not sufficient to encompass the subsequent developments in the sphere of action-naming. At present there is still a large performative element involved where action words are concerned: the child does not label some isolated object that he sees, but something he is at that moment doing and experiencing. This experiential aspect of early action-labelling is important: in most instances the child is both the actor and the patient with respect to the action at the focus of his attention. As adults we are able conceptually to disentangle actions and their effects. We distinguish between the active and passive effects of action, the action itself and the change of state that results from it, the experience of performing an action and the experience of being acted upon. It appears that the child cannot yet do this: in these early uses the word always occurs when he is both performing and experiencing the action at the same time.

Thus these early action words can be thought of as labels the child applies to his actual bodily experiences: the "concept" behind the use of the word differs from an adult conception of action. There is no distinction made by the child between subject, action and object because for him they are effectively all the same—he is the locus of the action, both its subject and its object at once. Further, he also seems to make no distinction between an action and the change in state that it engenders. But when he labels an action, not only does he experience that action bodily, he will also perceive the change in his circumstances occasioned by that action: not only does he experience, for example, "going down" he also perceives the results of this experience in the outside world—from "up there" to "down here".

Consequently, the semantic force of these early action-word utterances would appear to be best given as a highly complex one containing all the potential implicates of action which are later to be given expression by the child. This semantic force must also capture the almost totally undifferentiated concept of action that the child possesses at this time. To allow for all this it is proposed that the semantic force of action-labelling should be given not as THAT (IS) X_a but as:

(WHAT) (I AM DOING/EXPERIENCING) (THAT CHANGE IN STATE) (IS) THAT ACTION X_a (TO MYSELF)

In one sense this semantic force does not differ in nature from that of object-labelling, THAT (IS) X_o, in that both the subject and the object of it have identity. But it does differ, however, in that it is again an egocentric force, and does not thus attain to even the pseudo-propositional status of the object-naming utterance.

It is now possible to see why the child's use of action words is initially restricted to his own actions and not extended to those of others. Firstly, actions have no "objective" status for him in the sense that the physical objects he can name have. His conception of action is still very much tied to his experience of performing that action, and thus their status is more subjective than objective. Secondly, as a consequence of this, he possesses no true propositional structure to use action words within. That is, he cannot use utterances with the semantic force THAT (IS) X_a for the reasons stated above, nor within a force structured, say (YOU) (ARE DOING) X_a for those same reasons, *plus* the fact that he has yet to come to a true predicative ability—to be able to use an utterance with a semantic force in which the "subject" and "object" of that force are different objects. It is only through the incorporation of objects into an action-labelling act that action attains the necessary status for these abilities to emerge.

But while the semantic force ascribed to these early "action word" utterances—the inverted commas being necessitated by the ambiguous reference of these words: they only have a *potential* reference to what we as adults conceive actions to be—indicates that action words at first relate to the child's performance, it also points to the fact that they have in implicit purchase on the physical world. Future developments can then be conceived as the child's uncovering and making explicit these implications.

There is consequently a large chasm to be bridged before action words can move away from naming structures in which the child is implicated. That is, he has to create actions as objective entities, related to objects other than himself, distinguish actions from their effects; and so on. The fact that he is able to label his own performances is the first step in his process of creating the action as objective—it can exist as a word when it ceases to exist as a performance, and the child perhaps begins to develop a potentially objective structure such as (WHAT) (I AM DOING) (IS) X_a. The transformation of this possible structure into the objective from THAT (IS) X_a will be considered in the next chapter.

At this stage, then, the child possesses "language structures" as follows:

(1) (I) *WANT* THAT (volition)
(2) THAT (IS) X_o (object naming)
(3) (WHAT) (I AM DOING/EXPERIENCING)/(THAT CHANGE IN STATE) (IS) X_a (TO MYSELF) (early action-naming). That is, he can use words to *label* objects, and actions that he performs—he can *play* "language *games*" with his mother. But in terms of *"serious"* pursuits—the pursuit of his goals—he still relies on previously developed gestural strategies: his words are not yet used for this

purpose. In play he invents "words" which can only later be put to serious purposes.

Given these three abilities it becomes possible to advance certain hypotheses concerning the subsequent development of language. Firstly, it has already been possible to speculate that the act of naming an object might coalesce with a communicative gestural act, allowing the child to make a demand linguistically. Similarly, the possibility exists for the same development to occur with action words. Infants are capable of using arm-raising in order to enter into an action (cf. Lock, 1978). Thus, the possibility of their representing an intended action by a word is open to them. For further headway to be made in language, important developments must now be expected in the sphere of action-naming. For example, if it were possible to credit action-labelling with the structure $THAT$ (IS) X_a then the theoretical possibility of linguistic structures undergoing coalescence is opened up between this structure and that of, say, object naming, $THAT$ (IS) X_o, to yield X_o (IS) X_a or the more primitive (X_o) (IS) X_a $Teddy$ (IS) $DOWN$ or (Teddy) (IS) *down*. It would appear then that unless action-naming attains the structure THAT (IS) X_a the possibility of creating a speech act such as (X_o) (IS) X_a of predicating an action or state to an object, is not open to the child. To reach this structural status the labelled action must exist in an objective way; that is, the child must be able to use the action word in structures or initially situations, in which he is not implicated. An object which is named exists as a perceptually demarcated thing by its nature; an event has to be *created* with a similar existence prior to its being capable of constituting a structure such as THAT (IS) X_a—it does not possess this existence by nature. These expected developments of action-naming are discussed in Chapter 9. Before that, however, the beginnings of linguistic demands are discussed, this development probably being independent of any changes in the status of action words.

8.2 The insertion of words into demand structures

At the time the child develops the ability to name "objects" he is in possession of well-developed and productive gestural strategies. There emerges after what is perhaps a period of consolidation of the naming structure a new language use, that of using an object name as part of a request to be given that object (utterances used in this way are classified by Greenfield and Smith (1976) as volitional objects): an ability that has previously been accomplished solely by the use of gestures. This new ability, however, does not appear to be one that develops in the child's new linguistic system *de novo*. Rather it appears to arise through the coalescence of two older abilities, a process similar to that undergone earlier by the single gestures of crying and pointing: a coalescence of the gestural demand strategy with the child's object-naming linguistic ability.

If the structures given to these two abilities are juxtaposed, as in Fig. 8.9., then it might be expected that any coalescence would occur through pointing, which has a functional equivalence in both structures and thus effectively to the word $X_{o/a}$, being excluded, as shown in Fig. 8.10. But an inspection of Table 8.3 indicates that while coalescence certainly appears to be occurring, it is not occurring as was anticipated. Rather than the coalescence occurring by substitution as

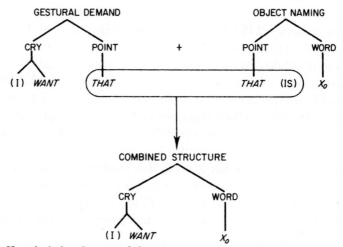

Fig. 8.9. Hypothetical coalescence of above two structures.

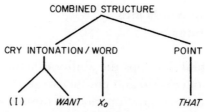

Fig. 8.10. Actual coalescence of gestural demand and object naming.

Table 8.3. Instances of volitional objects at Matthew V—17 (13).

Preceding context	Modality	Event
	M whining, repeats	*fishy*
	M whining, repeats	*fishy*
	M looking around for whining	bottle *bottle*
	M whining	*bottle*
Bananas are on table.	M pointing to whining	bananas *(ba)nana*
	M reaching for whining	banana *(ba)nana*
	M reaching up towards	mother *mommy*
	M whining, repeats	*(spaghett)io(s)*
Sitting on mother.	M whining, repeats	*cookie*
	M looking at mother whining, repeats	*cookie*
	M running and pointing to whining	record player *cacord, cacord* (record)
Record player is off	M running to	record player *record*
	M whining	*milk*
	M pointing to whining	door *door*
	M whining, repeats	*door*
Door is open	M whining	*door*

Table 8.3. (cont.)

Preceding context	Modality	Event
	M reaching for whining	refrigerator door *door*
	M reaching towards	drawer *drawer*

Note: Broken horizontal rules separate utterances that were not part of connected discourse. (From P. M. Greenfield and J. Smith, *The Structure of Communication in Early Language Development.* Reprinted by permission.)

in Fig. 8.10, what happens seems better represented by Fig. 8.11. In other words, while pointing and naming have an identity in labelling

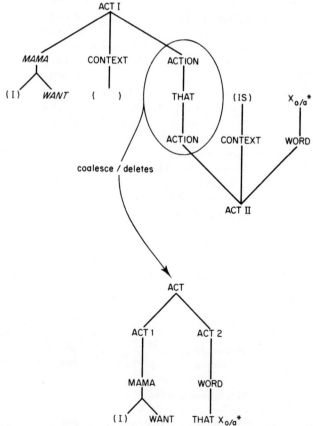

Fig. 8.11. Derivation of two-word demand utterance. *For explanation of $X_{o/a}$ see Section 9.2.3.

structures, gestural substitution does not occur by the replacement of pointing with a word having the equivalent function. Instead, the child combines crying with the word, so that the word is produced with a crying intonation—rather than crying and then using the word—and still points. This ability is illustrated in Table 8.3 which lists the early use of the linguistic object of demand structure by both Matthew and Nicky (from Greenfield *et al.*, 1972, data appendix). Action labels undergo a similar evolution, resulting in a structurally similar ability by which the child can demand actions. Table 8.4 illustrates this shift in

Table 8.4. Use of action of agent utterances in a demand context; Matthew III—15 (5) and 15 (7).

Preceding context	Modality	Event	
		M about to jump down stairs *down*	
Standing on the dishwasher, where he usually jumps down.		M *down*	
In high chair.	wh, r,	M trying to get down *down*	
In high chair.	wh, r	M trying to get down *down*	
In high chair.	wh, r	M trying to get down *down*	
	wh, r	M pulling and trying to get up on *down* (up)	chair
	wh, r	M pulling and trying to get up on *down* (up)	chair
	wh, r	M pulling and trying to get up on *down* (up)	chair

Note: Broken horizontal rules separate utterances that were not part of connected discourse. wh = whining; r = reaching.
(From P. M. Greenfield, J. Smith and B. Laufer (1972), *Communication and the Beginnings of Language*. by permission.)

use by Matthew from 14 (10) and 14 (18) to 15 (5) and 15 (17) (from Greenfield *et al.*, 1972).

Parenthetically, it is interesting to note that crying, at the same time that it is beginning to be used in combination with an object word to give a distinct intonation, is simultaneously undergoing development into the word *mama* (see Section 8.1.2). Thus there exists the possibility of a second similar structural coalescence to that just described, which, if it occurred, would result in the child exhibiting two-word speech: a coalescence in which the redundancy of pointing in an "object of demand" structure is finally realized by the child, pointing at last being excluded (see Fig. 8.12). This coalescence does occur, and is discussed in Section 10.1.

With respect to using object words in demands, Greenfield *et al.* (1972: 95) comment that:

> This type of demand emerges after the more general form *mama*. The delay is not due to lack of vocabulary, since a child can often label an object before he asks for it.

It would now appear that the different times at which these two modes of demand emerge is related to their developmental histories. The *mama*

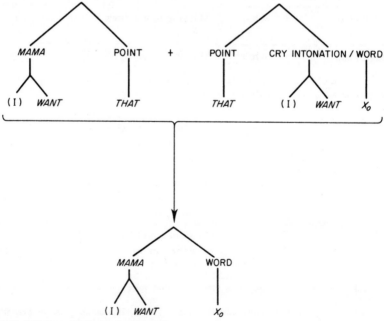

Fig. 8.12. Deletion of pointing in demands.

form appears directly from its gestural antecedent, whereas the object of demand form arises indirectly by a two-, not a one-, stage process.

At this stage, however, the child's early use of words is very restricted. He may label actions that he is performing and objects that solely exist; he may demand objects or "self-actions"; and no more. Yet he rapidly extends this ability, and he does so in such a way that both the manner and the speed of this extension indicate that it occurs by *spontaneous invention* on his part. The following chapter explores this possibility.

9. The extension of word use

9.1 Changes in the use of single words

The majority of contemporary studies adopt a semantic approach to
early child language, making much use of the notions of agent, actor,
action, object, dative and so on (e.g. Braine, 1976; Greenfield and
Smith, 1976; Ingram, 1971; Leonard, 1976; Ramer, 1975; Schlesinger,
1974; Slobin, 1970, 1972). Brown (1973: 200) suggests a relationship
exists between the development of these semantic notions and the
child's sensori-motor capabilities.

> Agent, object, datives of indirect object, and person affected construc-
> tions if they are used in a freely combinatorial way, with the names of
> referents playing one role on one occasion and another on another,
> presuppose the knowledge that the self, other persons, and objects are all
> potentially "sources of causality" or initiators of forces and also, poten-
> tially, recipients of forces. Piaget judges this knowledge to be entirely
> lacking in the early sensori-motor stages. One can see that it has begun to
> evolve when the child tries to move the hand of an adult or set off some
> skilled action beyond his own agentive capacity. But a reasonably objec-
> tive sense of causality does not evolve until the fifth stage.
>   In sum, I think that the first sentences express the construction of
> reality which is the terminal achievement of sensori-motor intelligence.
> What has been acquired on the plane of motor intelligence (the perma-
> nence of form and substance of immediate objects) and the structure of
> immediate space and time does not need to be formed all over again on the

plane of representation. Representation starts with just those meanings that are most available to it, propositions about action-schemas involving agents and objects, assertions of non-existence, recurrence, location and so on. But representation carries intelligence beyond the sensori-motor. Representation is a new level of operation which quickly moves to meanings that go beyond immediate space and practical action.

Little emphasis has been given thus far to the existence of a knowledge in the child's pre-language phase that could be described in these terms. But with the demonstration that certain aspects of the child's emerging use of language can be traced right back to some of his earliest transactions with the world—for example, using referential language to demand an object—Brown's comments appear most attractive. In the same way that the child learning the words of his language does not have to learn simultaneously how to communicate, likewise he does not have to create the concepts that underlie the words he is acquiring—he has already created, at least in outline, the concept of, say, an agent in developing the ability to use gestures for intentional communication (see Chapter 5) and thus at this time he merely has to learn a word that refers to that concept. The obvious parallel that exists between this scheme for the roots of referential word usage and that already advanced for communicative word usage makes it a proposition which has found favour among many current writers who are seeking to explore the relationship between sensori-motor knowledge and language development (e.g. Bates *et al.*, 1975; Bates, 1976; Dore, 1973; Edwards, 1973; Ingram, 1975, 1978; MacNamara, 1972; Morehead and Morehead, 1974; Sinclair, 1973, 1975; Sugarman, 1973). Bloom (1973: 16), for example, comes very close to Brown's view when she says "children learn language as a linguistic coding of developmentally prior conceptual representations of experience".

However, the attraction of these views can lead to a clouding of some fundamental issues. Certainly, prior to language the child is developing a form of knowledge, of which facets could be described from a common-sense perspective in terms like agent, dative and so on. But the relation of these terms to what "the first sentences express" is a different matter. This can be appreciated both from a theoretical viewpoint, and one which considers the ways in which single-word utterances come to be used by the child.

From the theoretical perspective being developed here, two of Brown's points are suspect straightaway. The first of these is his claim that "representation starts with . . . propositions about . . .". As has already been argued, prior to the emergence of language, that is during the period in which he is credited only with sensori-motor knowledge, the young infant does not possess a propositional ability. Consequently the suggestion that representation begins with propositions about sensori-motor knowledge misses the crucial question of where that ability comes from, how "the terminal achievement of sensori-motor intelligence" comes about.

Secondly, and more importantly, Brown's comments also suggest that once this propositional ability has been acquired, the child can make propositions about all manner of things because he already possesses the necessary concepts in a sufficiently developed form, thus "representation is a new level of operation . . .". Reading between the lines, Brown seems to be saying that the child in the fifth stage of sensori-motor knowledge possesses an objective enough sense of causality to be able to make propositions about schemata involving agents and objects once he acquires a few referential words. But it has been argued here that objectivity only develops through the possession of language. What might actually be meant, then, by a *"reasonably* objective sense of causality"? This is an important question, for while Brown's opinion—that "the first sentences express the construction of reality which is the terminal achievement of sensori-motor intelligence"—is untenable—these "terminal achievements" not being sufficient to allow the propositional usage of representational speech—there is a certain degree of plausibility in his views.

This "degree of plausibility" can be determined by considering the changes in use of referential single-word utterances as the child's language abilities develop. This topic is discussed more fully in the remainder of this chapter, but it is worth anticipating that discussion by thinking about Mary's behaviour in Observation 60, where she attempts to grasp something beyond her reach, fails, attracts her mother's attention and then uses a gesture to communicate successfully her previously frustrated intention. There can be little dispute that to act in this way Mary possesses, in Brown's terms "the knowledge that the self, other persons, and objects are all potentially 'sources of causality' or initiators of forces and also, potentially, recipients of forces". Thus notions such as agent, object, datives of indirect object and the like, which presuppose this knowledge, certainly come into play. That they do is illustrated by the fact that the semantic force (I) *WANT* (YOU GIVE ME) *THAT* can be confidently applied to her actions. What has to be ascertained is how they come into play.

The semantic force is expressed in terms of components from a system of objective knowledge: and Mary does not possess such a system, instead her knowledge exists in the sensori-motor dimension. Thus the semantic force given to Mary's actions, and notions such as agent, object and so on are really only *implicit* in those actions; their force is completed by the adult recipient of them. Brown's statement should thus be rewritten as follows: the first sentences express—i.e. *make explicit*—the construction of reality which is *implicit in* the terminal achievement of sensori-motor intelligence. Objective notions such as agent, object and so on are cultural products, and only exist implicitly in the prespeech child's behaviour. (And consequently some of them need never be made explicit: the semantic force I AM HUNGRY is certainly implicit in many infant cries, implying potential concepts of self and being. But in Eskimo language, for example, there are no words for self and no forms of the verb "to be" (Carpenter, 1966). What is implicit in the Eskimo child's activities is never made explicit in his culture.) To ascribe to such a child the possession of the concept "agent" is a fundamental error: what can be said is that the child interacts with the world in ways which he *could* come to conceive of in objective terms—such as agent or object—reached through a creative process of *guided reinvention* in which the individuals who act as enculturating agents for the child guide his spontaneous reflective abilities along the path of making explicit in an acceptable fashion what is already implicit in his actions.

But this creative development must not be thought of as occurring in a social vacuum: *it is not an unfolding of an individual ability.* Ryan (1974: 205), in discussing the "interpretative approach" to the study of early child language—the approach used here—notes that those using this approach have tended to

> conflate the means . . . by which an adult interprets a child's utterances with the devices it is assumed a child uses to express herself, given her limitation to the one word form. That is, they assume a child uses the same devices to convey her meaning as an adult uses in interpreting the utterance. The question arises of whether we can in principle tell if such an assumption is correct or not. In some cases we can tell with some confidence if we are wrong in our interpretations (for example, if we do something we think is appropriate and the child screams); however, very often we cannot. . . . It is possible that what is most important for the child is not whether she is correctly interpreted by adults, but that she is interpreted at all. The context of rich interpretation provided by many

F

mothers, combined with the considerable ambiguity of many one-word utterances, provides an extremely informative situation for the child as regards what she is taken to be meaning. We cannot assume when a child starts to produce one-word utterances, that the possible meanings of her utterances are as clearly delimited for her as they are for the adults who interpet them.

The view that must be taken, then, of this period in which the child is extending his new language ability is that it is often both pointless and fruitless to ask what a particular utterance means. Rather, it is a case of taking the whole situation in which the utterance occurs, considering the way the mother interprets the utterance and reflects back this interpretation to the child in her subsequent actions: of looking at the utterance and its consequences as part of a process whereby the mother and child *negotiate* what the utterance *might* mean, and not attempting to say categorically what it *does* mean.

As a concrete example, take Nicky's use of the word *truck* in Observation session VI, age 22 (22) (Greenfield and Smith, 1976: 124). The context of the utterance is reported as "mother has made a truck" and Nicky says the word *truck*. This utterance is classified as an Object of Direct Action. But, this classification is difficult to substantiate. Ryan's comments (above) on the tendency of researchers to conflate the means by which adult and child interpret the meaning of an utterance are well illustrated in this case. Certainly from the adult point of view the truck is an object of direct action, but is there any justification in assuming that this state of affairs is perceived by the child? Could it not be that he is ignoring the situation and is simply labelling the truck? Well obviously he could be. And if the truck is only labelled by the child because it, and nothing else, is the focus of his attention, classifying the utterance as an instance of one grammatical case or another become incidental: "grammar" in fact begins to look like an artifact.

But if these early utterances are approached from a developmental perspective and analysed in terms of act-structures, then their indeterminate nature presents us with less of a conceptual problem. *Truck* can in this framework be thought of as a *potential* case of the utterance of an Object of Direct Action by the child. If it is viewed as a component of a communicative act made by the child its indeterminate status can be sensibly encompassed (see Fig. 9.1). The meaning of the utterance is context dependent, and since there is no way of knowing whether it is made within an agreed context or not, it is fruitless to ask what its exact meaning is. Yet it is, however, open to the mother and child to agree

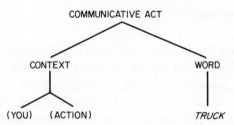

Fig. 9.1. See text for explanation.

upon the context. By coming to this agreement the utterance has its potentiality realized, and the child becomes truly capable of referring to the objects of direct actions. Thus through the making of a social agreement the child comes to possess a new cognitive ability.

In sum, then, the perspective here is that the child in developing his first referential ability acquires means by which he can begin to make explicit many of the things that must implicitly exist in his knowledge.

9.2 The development of word usage from the initial bases of object- and action-labelling

Before providing any evidence in support of the argument to be discussed in this section, I shall first describe the nature of the argument in broad terms. It is now fairly well-established that a process of decentring occurs during the "holophrastic" period. At first the child refers only to objects he is acting upon. Gradually he comes to refer to the actions of others and also to the objects on which they act. I wish to argue that this shift reflects a shift from non-propositional usage to propositional usage. At first the child is merely announcing intentions, demands or continuing actions, but not making statements. Further I shall argue that this transition is a conceptual transition which depends upon the child's ability to conceive of actions and events beyond his own personal sphere of action. Finally, I shall argue that this conceptual transition is brought about by the language function itself. In the course of very early language use the child provides himself with the means whereby he can make explicit what is already implicit in his abilities, and thus provides himself with the conceptual apparatus for eventually making a proposition. Hence language may depend upon thought, but thought in turn depends upon language.

9.2.1 The problem and the data

The problem I am discussing in the next few sections is this. With the emergence of object- and action-labelling the child establishes language, but not a propositional ability. In the case of object-labelling the child relates an object to itself and not to another object: in that of action-labelling he relates an action he is performing—either its physical or experiential consequences—to himself, and he is not yet an object in his own perceptions. To progress from this position to being able to refer to an object another acts upon, or that action another is performing requires two developments. Firstly, the ability to relate one object to another—an ability he implicitly possesses in the sensori-motor domain—must be realized productively in his linguistic capacities. Secondly, he must disentangle the experiential and physical consequences of actions, and make the distinction between an agent, the action performed and the result of that action (at least in our culture). In sum he must make a transition to objective forms of knowledge.

Thus early in his language development he might be able to say *down* when he is in the process of going down, but never when he sees his mother going down. To do this would require him to relate an event to an object other than himself—his mother—to make a proposition, and to conceive actions in a propositional way. He does not initially possess either of these abilities. The problem is, then, where do these abilities come from. We can either assume that they emerge *de novo*, or that they have direct links with earlier abilities: I assume the latter. Consequently the following sections attempt to establish what these links are, and how the child realizes them for himself. In doing this I will draw on the data corpus of Greenfield *et al.* (1972, 1976) to give the discussion some purchase on reality. However, my purpose is not to explain the course of language development in any particular child, but rather to gain a general understanding of the basic processes underlying language development itself. To this end certain aspects of this particular data corpus have been distorted, i.e. simultaneous developments have been treated as constituting distinct episodes.

These distortions are introduced for the sake of simplicity. The intention is to show how one language ability is logically implicated in the appearance of another, and it simplifies matters in doing this to assume that the child consolidates one ability before he progresses from this basis to the next. This assumption is, however, unwarranted. For example, it will emerge that utterances that can be described as labelling Inanimate Objects of Direct Action occupy a very important place in the course of language development. The ability to make such utterances is a springboard for the appearance of many new abilities. But the problem of knowing when an utterance actually constitutes an instance that can be classified in this way has already been referred to above in the case of Nicky's use of the word *truck* (Section 9.1). *Truck* perhaps marks the beginning of this usage, and it will not be for some time that this ability is consolidated. But the developments which hinge upon this ability do not wait for this consolidation to be finalized: they begin while their parent ability is still emerging—the roof is begun before the walls are finished. Yet to take account here of this state of affairs would further complicate the task in hand: thus it is ignored.

The first extension of object-labelling is to objects that are implicated in the child's own activities—he begins to name the objects of his own acts. In labelling these objects he is creating knowledge of them which differs from that which he has previously possessed: it is knowledge which is focused upon features of the objects of *his actions in independence of his states*. Further in extending his labelling ability to encompass objects he is acting upon he consolidates this "non-affective" knowledge. His actions become related more to the object than to himself, he begins to perceive his actions in relation to the object he acts upon, not his own bodily state; and similarly the object in relation to the action. The only way in which the child is implicated in the structure of this form of knowledge is through his being the agent performing the action upon that object: his knowledge begins to take on an objective character as it is affectively value free.

Concerning this development Greenfield *et al.* (1972: 116) note "Inanimate Objects of Direct Action become very numerous at Nicky II—18 (27)—occurring twelve times with seven objects names and seven actions. They remain numerous throughout". However, Objects of Action in which Nicky has no part do not become frequent until Observation session VI—22 (21)—and is still the verbalization of the objects of his own acts which predominate throughout. Why might this be? The answer I suggest is that the ability to talk about the objects of other people's actions is developmentally advanced and complex. Thus in the early stages of his development Nicky restricts his utterances to objects of his own actions because using his language to describe another acting on that object would require a propositional ability he does not yet possess.

Further, I suggest that the following sequence of development in Nicky's language is not arbitrary, but fixed:

(1) *Prior to Observation session II,* 18 (27), Nicky is able to:
 (a) label objects;
 (b) label some of his own actions;
 (c) use these words in the pursuit of his own intentions.

(2) *At the time of session II* he evidences three new abilities, being able to use utterances labelling:
 (a) certain *actions he performs* on inanimate objects, or actions he performs when an object other than himself is implicated in that performance—for example, *down* while pulling his train down;
 (b) *the state of certain objects;* for example, *on* while pointing at a light which is switched on;
 (c) *the inanimate objects of his own direct actions;* for example, *milk* when he picks up a glass of milk; *bap* when he picks up his diaper.

(3) *After session II* he labels:
 (a) certain *actions that others perform;* whether upon an object or not; for example *bang* when Matthew bangs his head (session VI, 22, (22)); this ability is established by the time of session VI, 22 (22);
 (b) again in session VI, 22 (22), *the inanimate objects of other people's direct actions;* for example, *bed* when mother is making the bed; *potatoes* when she is putting them in a dish.

My major argument, then, is, that this sequence of development could not occur in any other order, and that each new ability has definite antecedents in the child's previous abilities, which determine the sequence by their conjoint natural implicates.

9.2.2 The transition to naming objects being acted on by the child and also the actions themselves

The assumption here is that when in session II Nicky labels an object he is acting upon, his focus of attention is not yet only the object, but the whole situation that the object is immersed in. Thus it is not possible to ascribe the semantic force of earlier object labelling—$THAT$ (IS)X_0—to these utterances: rather the force should be one which includes the action being performed as well. In making this assumption it is possible to see why only objects of self actions, and not those of others, are labelled at this time. Firstly, the child's conception of action is still very much tied up with his own performance and experience of them; and secondly, he cannot yet predicate an event to an object. In grammatical terms this second point is that the child cannot announce an object as the subject of some underlying proposition, but only as an object "predicated" to himself.

In terms of semantic forces this means that these utterances cannot yet be represented by, say, THAT X_0 (IS BEING PUSHED) ... because the child cannot yet conceive actions or changes in state in the necessary objective manner: he cannot relate an object to an "objective event" since they do not exist for him. But what he can do is relate an object to himself and his own non-objective performance: he does this already when he uses an object word as part of a demand. Thus we may fairly ascribe a semantic force such as (I) (AM DOING ACTION TO) X_0 to these utterances. The present problem then, is to account for the transition from using object words with their initial labelling force to their later predicative one.

Resolving this problem requires attention to be turned for a moment away from objects and towards actions. Prior to session II Nicky could label his own actions as he performed them, and thus it was suggested that his action words had a large experiential component. They have at the same time, however, a physical component: the child not only experiences the action, but also sees its physical result. Further, he can use action words in demands.

These three abilities—to name an object, an action, and to make a small distinction between subjective and objective correlates of the effects of actions—are sufficient in combination to allow the child to make the next development in his language inevitable. Now when he looks at an object he is acting upon he perceives a situation in which he has some conception of the object's movement, some conception of the object's having a name, and he is also the actor. He could begin to explicitly distinguish the object-as-patient from the action it suffers: but not directly from this basis the subject-as-actor from the action performed. He does not, however, need to do this to label an object he is acting upon, nor the action he is performing. Consequently, *only* these utterances make an appearance at this time. The three earlier abilities are sufficient to allow just this much development, and no more.

In terms of semantic forces the following may be said. From using words with the semantic forces of:

(1) (I) *WANT* X_a;

(2) *THAT* (IS) X_0; and

(3) (WHAT) (I AM DOING/EXPERIENCING) (IS) (THAT

CHANGE IN STATE) (IS) X_a (TO MYSELF);

he can move to using them within the force:

(4) (WHAT) (I AM DOING/EXPERIENCING) (IS) (THAT
CHANGE IN STATE) (IS)

X_a (TO) X_a (– – denoting either one or the other element is verbalized).

He can do this because his three earlier abilities, (1), (2) and (3), are
sufficient in combination to allow him to; *(4) is implied by (1), (2) and (3)
through conjoint natural implication, and is now explicated.*

9.2.3 The transition to naming objects acted upon by another and also the actions themselves: the emergence of the proposition

It is the development of these two new abilities, to name objects he acts
on and the resulting changes the object undergoes or the action he
performs upon it, that is crucial for the child to attain to the propositional level of language. Just as his three previous abilities allowed him
to move to these two new ones, so these in turn open up the possibility of
further developments. Mead comments that:

> Symbolisation constitutes objects not constituted before, objects which
> would not exist except for the context of social relationships wherein
> symbolisation occurs. Language does not simply symbolise a situation or
> object which is already there in advance; it makes possible the existence or
> the appearance of that situation or object, for it is a part of the mechanism
> whereby that situation or object is created.   (Mead, 1934: 78)

The symbolization inherent in naming an object or the action performed on it effects this function of "constituting objects not constituted
before". The child's knowledge of action is now not only structured
around himself, but also around the objects he acts upon. This
development is sufficient to open up the possibility of action becoming
anchored around objects *per se*. Action can now be constituted as
something explicitly conceived in independence of an experienced
performance. An alternative way of looking at this change is through
the semantic forces involved. He can now use action words with either:

(1) (WHAT) (I AM DOING/EXPERIENCING) (IS) (THAT
CHANGE IN STATE) (IS) X_a (TO) (MYSELF)

or

(2) (WHAT (I AM DOING/EXPERIENCING) (IS) (THAT

CHANGE IN STATE) (IS) X_a (TO) X_o.

These two forces in conjunction open up the possibility of his perceiving both the changes in state he experiences and those he causes an object to undergo as instances of the same explicit event; he can now potentially relate, or predicate, changes in state not only to himself, but also to objects. That is, these explicit semantic forces have as a conjoint natural implicate one which has a propositional nature: my doing something to an object (non-propositional) implies that the object is having something done to it (propositional). This potentiality is quickly actualized, and the child begins to label objects which are being acted upon irrespective of the actor. Nicky begins to do this immediately during session II, 18 (28), but the ability is not consolidated for some time: and even then Greenfield *et al.* (1972: 116) note "the verbalisation of objects of his own acts, rather than those of others, predominates throughout". Similarly, "not until Nicky, VI—22 (21)—does the encoding of Action Performed by an Agent other than Nicky become productive"(1972: 111), but prior to this time there is evidence that the ability is emerging.

Unfortunately, there is an additional complication at this point. Greenfield and Smith (1976: 122) note Harris' suggestion that what children attend to is change. Thus the components of change, the action and its result are undifferentiated aspects of a more basic event. Consequently, in the same way that a child has to come to distinguish an actor from the actions he performs, he also has to come to distinguish those actions from their results. This is largely common sense, and has been anticipated in the complex semantic force ascribed to early action utterances. It becomes necessary on this view, then, to regard the development of the propositional ability as dependent on the child's emerging conception of the components of change.

Utterances relevant to this topic made by Nicky I–III, 18(4)–19(29) are listed in Table 9.1. At first sight it would appear that these utterances must be propositional by definition: but on reflection it appears that this is not so. Firstly, many of the early utterances classed under this heading could equally well refer to actual perceptual events as opposed to being predications of states to objects. For example, the utterance *on* used by Nicky in both sessions II and III, firstly with relation to light and secondly to tape-recorder: also *round* again with respect to the tape-recorder.

Secondly, it will be remembered that the child can already use action words in demands, for example Matthew uses *down* as a request in

Table 9.1. Instances of action or state of inanimate object/utterances.

Preceding context	Modality		Event	
(a) *Nicky 1*: 18 (4)	N reaching for		hot *hot*	soup
(b) *Nicky 2*: 18 (27) N is holding book upside down. *Do you want to read it upside down?*		book	is upside down *down*	
N is holding book upside down.		book	is upside down *down*	
		record	is playing *ong*	
A piece broke off.		piece of cheese	has broken off *b*(rok)*e*(n)	
	wh N pointing to light		is on *on*	
		N	pulled down his train *down*	
N has finished his juice.	N wh	*mou* (more)		
	N looking at	picture of	big *bi bi bi*	dogs
Did it break?		cheese	has broken *bai*	
	N looking at	book	about apples *ael*	
	N pulling	his pants	*poo*	
		mother takes off record	that starts with "hi" *hi*	

Preceding context	Modality		Event
		mother puts on record	that starts with "hi" *hi*
(c) *Nicky 3*: 19 (29)	N pointing to cup		has dropped *dop* (used twice in this context)
	N pointing to nut		has dropped *dop*
N has seen tape recorder going round.	r N goes to see tape-recorder go round		*round*
	wh N pointing to tape- recorder *on*		(used twice in this context)
N has finished playing with water.	r	bib	is on *on* (off)
		N	takes down cup *down*
		N	gives back plate to mother *back*
N is drinking from cup.		cup	is hot *hot*
(d) *Matthew 6*: 18 (18) *Where is the car going?*			*by-by*

Table 9.1 *(Cont)*

Preceding context	Modality		Event
What happened?		stove	has pieces missing *broke*
		cars	*gone*
The record is up here		record	*gone*
		airplane	flying overhead *gone*
	M looking into	beaker	empty *gone*
		ring toy	has no rings on it *gone*
Milk carton has been empty	M pointing to	milk carton	is now full *gone*
Where's the juice?	M holds up	glass	empty *gone*
	M pointing to	his skate	*on*
		ceiling light	going in circle *round and round* (used twice in this context)
What is record doing?	M. making circular motion with hand & pointing to	record	going round *round and round*
	M watching	mother	pull up buggy *down* (up)

Preceding context	Modality		Event	
	M		pulling down buggy *down*	
	M		takes off *gone*	pieces from toy
	M		about to pushcar *byebye*	
	M		pushing *byebye*	car
Now put it back	M reaching for	food container	to put back *back*	
	M looking at	record player	is turned on *on*	
What are they doing?	M		spinning round toy rings *round and round*	
	M		throws down *down*	car
	M		patting	his car *beepbeep*
	M		picks up	another ring *more*
	wh M points to		*more*	fish food
M has heard cars outside	wh M looking for		*more*	cars
	wh M hands	mother	broken *broke*	piece

Table 9.1(cont.)

Preceding context	Modality	Event	
		dirty diaper is being removed *dirty*	
	M pointing to	dirty *dirty*	finger
	M looking at	hot *hot*	cereal
	M points to	*poop*	his penis
	M	touching	diaper *poop*
	M	clutching	diaper *poop*

Note: Broken horizontal rules separate utterances that were not part of connected discourse.
wh = whining; r = reaching.
(From P. M. Greenfield, J. Smith and B. Laufer (1972), *Communication and the Beginnings of Language*. By permission.)

session III (see Table 8.5). Likewise,

> at the time of the first formal observation 18 (4), Nicky says *up* while reaching up to the fan. Thus one could say that the Action word *up* is embedded in a demand context expressed through the reach, a familiar performative element in the expression of the Demand Modality. Thus the Action word *up* is now part of a more complicated action structure involving both demand and description of action.
>
> (Greenfield *et al.*, 1972)

As noted above, these uses imply a potential objective conception of "place" or state—the child is "recognizing" some "abstract" quality. But he is not necessarily relating this quality to another object, he could be relating it to himself: i.e. *up* (is above me), *down* (is below me). This would allow him to use utterances that appear to relate to objects, but perhaps relate an object's position to himself. For example in session II, 18 (27) (see Table 9.1) "Nicky pulled his train down and said *down*. Although Nicky is the Agent, it is the *resultant action* of the object that is coded rather than his own" (Greenfield *et al.*, 1972). Or perhaps it is the resultant position of the object with respect to himself; the utterance is very vague and the object is only accessory to it.

In these cases it is not only unnecessary to consider the utterance to be propositional, but there is also another important factor involved. Early in the history of this class of utterance there are many "states of objects" that the child apparently comments on which are more likely to be expressions of relationships between him and his experiences, and not between an object and its state. A clear example would be Matthew's utterance *cold* in session IV, 16 (2) (see Table 9.2). In their corpus Greenfield *et al.* (1972) relate *cold* to the air which Matthew felt, suggesting thus the semantic force THAT (AIR) (IS) *COLD*. An alternative force would be THAT (EXPERIENCE/FEELING) (IS) *COLD*. The utterance then relates the child to the "object" through his experience of it, and not the object to its state.

Initially, then, these utterances may not differ in their semantic force from ordinary object-naming: the child is saying of some event or experience that that event is that event in the same way as he was saying that that object is that object. It is only later that objects become implicated in the utterances which consequently become propositional: it is only later that experiences are objectified as properties of objects. "Heaviness" for example, would in this way be seen first as a facet of the experience of picking up an object and only later as a property of that object. States and Actions of Inanimate objects have to be "decentred" in much the same way as other functions of speech. Further, this decentration develops hand-in-hand with that occurring in the sphere of naming objects being acted upon. The child's language ability there engenders a change in his perception such that his attention when acting upon an object is equally divided between his experience of his acting and the consequences of his action upon the object: he begins to distinguish actions from their effects. The development of "state" utterances is merely the other side of this coin. In the first case he begins to name the object being acted upon—changed in state— irrespective of the actor; in the second, he moves to naming the change in state.

Table 9.2. Instances of action or state of inanimate object/utterances Matthew IV—16
(2)

Preceding context	Modality	Event		
Do you make car go byby?		car which M was playing with	*byby*	
The window was up and closed.	wh, r M looking at	window	*down* (wants open)	
	M looking at	car	going away *byby*	
	M pointing to	car	going away *byby*	
		outside where M was looking	cold *cold*	
		outside where M was standing	cold *cold*	
It's cold out there.		air which M felt	cold *cold*	
It's cold out there.		air which M felt	cold *cold*	

Note: Broken horizontal rules separate utterances that were not part of connected discourse.
wh = whining; r = reaching.
(From P. M. Greenfield, J. Smith and P. Laufer (1972), *Communication and the Beginnings of Language.* By permission.)

It was noted above that the development of both the ability to name an object being acted upon irrespective of the actor, and to name actions in this way, was complicated by developments in the present sphere of action or state of inanimate objects. The complication is this: both these former abilities are propositional in nature, and this is the function which the child has to develop. It is accomplished during this period of objectifying changes in state through the mediation of objects acted upon: the suggestion was that the child's attention becomes divided between his action and the object, and thus moves progressively to the object itself. He develops the ability to predicate "state" to objects, a development which can be seen occurring in Table 9.1 for Nicky's utterances, and is illustrated in its fully developed form in the same table for Matthew in session VI, 18 (18). The focus of attention appears to be the object *per se,* and only rarely is another action or agency implicated in the situation being referred to. This also appears to be the case when it comes to utterances referring to the objects of direct actions when the child is not the agent: the change in state of the object—the object as the subject of a proposition—is attended to, rather than the action performed on the object–the object as predicated to another's actions. This can be seen for Matthew in Table 9.3. The implication of this is that the child is consolidating his perception of the distinction between an action and its effects by focusing on an object. This would explain why Greenfield and Smith (1976: 138) conclude that in practise, both Matthew and Nicky develop the ability to express the *Action or State* of an Object after they have expressed the *Object* of an Action (but see Section 9.2.1.), whereas I am suggesting that the appearance of utterances encoding the objects of direct actions and the actions performed on those objects would be simultaneous. Action or State utterances may be that much more propositional in nature and thus require more gestation.

At this point it becomes possible to spell out and clarify these arguments by looking at the developments noted in terms of the semantic forces involved. The starting point is the clumsy and baroque force ascribed to early utterances tied up with the performance of some activity, viz:

(a) (WHAT) (I AM DOING/EXPERIENCING) (IS) (THAT CHANGE IN STATE) (IS) X_a (TO MYSELF).

Discussed above is how in conjunction with the ability to name objects THAT (IS) X_o—the child becomes able to move on to many objects he acts upon, or the actions he performs upon them (or their change in state, which is conceptually the same thing for the child at this point):

(b) (WHAT) (I AM DOING/EXPERIENCING) (IS) (THAT CHANGE IN STATE) (IS) X_a (TO) X_o

Similarly, in utterances which appear to us as adults to have more relation to the actual states of objects than the actions performed upon

Table 9.3. Instances of inanimate object of direct action/utterances

Preceding context	Modality		Event
(a) *Matthew 3*:15 (5) and 15 (17)			
	M	picks up	spool of ribbon *kaka*
	M	picks up	his shoe *sh*
	M	picks up	a round bead *ball*
	M	throws	the ball *ball*
The ball has rolled under the couch.	M	looking for	the ball *ball*
	M	pushing	button on tape-recorder *ba*
What's that?	M	patting	his tummy bap (belly button)
	M	gives	spoon to mother *spoon*
	M	goes to start	record player *crecor*
(b) *Matthew 4*: 16 (2)			
	M	trying to push	button on wall *ba*
	M	trying to push	button on wall *ba*
	M	going to turn on	light *light*

Preceding context	Modality	Event	
	M	turns on	light *light*
	M	turns on	light *light*
	M	turns off	light *light*
	M	takes from shelf	car *car*
	M	putting on	bottle top *top*
	M	drinking *ju*	juice
	M	about to close *door*	door
	M	trying to open	refrigerator door *door*
Crayons have fallen	M	looking for	crayons *craw*
	M	has closed	door *door*
M looking at mother		playing with	crayons *craw*
	M	eating with	spoon *poon*
M looking at crayon box is empty			*craw*

Table 9.3 (cont.)

Preceding context	Modality	Event
	M pointing to crayons	have fallen
		craw

Preceding context	Modality	Event
M has left room where		light is off
		light

---

		his book has fallen
		book

	M is closing	door hurt his finger
		door

	M pointing to crayons	just dropped by M
		craw

Note: Broken horizontal rules separate utterances that were not part of connected discourse. wh = whining; r = reaching.
(From P. M. Greenfield, J. Smith and B. Laufer (1972), *Communication and the Beginnings of Language*. By permission.)

them, it is possible to perceive a similar "decentring" of the semantic force away from the child towards an object. For example, during their first formal observation session Nicky, 18 (4), Greenfield and Smith (1976: 114) report an occurrence of the utterance *hot*.

> Nicky says *hot* while starting to eat hot soup. This type of usage has been classed as Action or State of Agent rather than object because the child changes state to hot. If this were a description of the object, it would represent a constant-State description, a development that occurs much later.

To this utterance may be given the slightly more complex semantic force than that introduced above in the case of *cold*:

(c) (THAT) (EXPERIENCE/FEELING) (IS) X_s (VIA X_o)

where (VIA X_o) indicates the object implied in the situation underlying the use of the utterance. Later (1976: 131),

> between 19 (8) and 19 (15), Nicky began saying *(h)ot*. while blowing on cooked food. Here, the fact that Nicky is blowing on, rather than eating, the food constitutes behavioural evidence that he is referring to the Object's State rather than his own.

In ascribing a semantic force to this utterance it is necessary to emphasize both the relation of the word *hot* to an object, and also the fact that it is linked to the child's (as opposed to another's) interaction with the object. Hence my suggestion of the force:

(d) (THAT) (EXPERIENCE/FEELING) (IS) X_s (VIA) X_o

Now these semantic forces all have an object firmly implicated in them. Whilst I find it impossible to spell out the process at work here, it is possible to grasp intuitively the fact that since the child's focus of attention is becoming progressively decentred to include these implied objects, then the following semantic forces become more plausibly attributable to his utterances as the conjoint natural implicates of their actual semantic forces. Firstly for b above we have:

(e) X_o (IS DOING/CHANGING IN STATE) X_a

Secondly for (c) and (d) above we have:

(f) X_o (IS) X_s.

Thus we find utterances coming more and more to reflect these conjoint semantic forces. Decentration occurs through the child making explicit the conjoint natural implicates of earlier forces such that he can make the transition to talking about objects and events involved in the activities of others. Further, it should be noted that he has now explicated the propositional level of function.

The argument can now be shifted to further facets of the child's language development, for the conjoint natural implicate of force (e) above—X_o (IS DOING/CHANGING IN STATE) X_a/X_s—is (AGENT) (IS ACTING ON) X_o. These present disentanglements of the facets of action, its results and states by the child, with their concomitant production of the propositional function should provide a sufficient base for the emergence of agent and action-of-other-agent utterances.

9.2.4 Action-labelling: the emergence of agent and action-of-other-agent utterances

In making demands, and in labelling the action or state of inanimate objects, the child necessarily begins to implicate the other as agent in the semantic forces of his utterances. This also occurs when he names the inanimate object of a direct action where he is not the actor. For example, in the case of the productive semantic force (I) *WANT* THAT X_o there exists as a conjoint natural implicate (YOU) (GIVE) (TO ME) THAT X_o. Similarly, for the force THAT (IS) X_o (IS DOING/

EXPERIENCING) (X_a) there is often the implicate (YOU) (ARE DOING X_a) to X_o. Naming actions that another performs is an ability that has been alluded to above. Here I will concentrate on the factors that underlie the emergence of Agent utterances and thus deal with the former utterances by default—they appear to become productive at the same time as Agent utterances, and thus remarks concerning one may be directly applied to the other.

The first object-naming word used correctly by both Matthew and Nicky was *dada* (this was not fortuitous, but was the result of a deliberate attempt by Greenfield to influence the child's language development as part of a replication of an earlier study, Greenfield, 1973). A word for Mother was also established early on. Thus both children actually possessed words that could be used in agentive ways, but have been unable to do so. Now, as a result of the developments in object and "action" labelling discussed above they possess the propositional ability necessary to allow them to both form an objective concept of agency and give that concept linguistic expression. This notion of "an ability to form an objective concept of agency" is a peculiar one. Its meaning can be brought out in the following way. In Nicky's case, propositional acts appear to be fully fledged by Observation session VI, age 22 (21), and it is in this session that he first uses words to refer to Agents. It might thus be argued that at the time of this session Nicky already possessed a concept of Agent, and that its expression has merely been waiting upon the development of the necessary vehicle, the proposition. But this argument, plausible as it is, misses an important aspect of language development: that Nicky, in this case, only has *implicit* possession of that concept: it requires language to make it explicit, to create it as an actual concept. Many domestic animals have such implicit concepts of agency, but we need not credit them with *actually possessing* that concept.

Consider again the case of frustrated crying. There the child begins by expressing a negative attitude to some occurrence, and implying by default a potential positive attitude to some other state of affairs. In a similar vein, the concept of Agent *may* be thought of as developing by default. The child has been coming to a more and more objective conception of action immediately prior to this point in time: where initially he made no distinction between object, action and resultant change in state in his utterances he now does so. In drawing these distinctions in his perceptual world he leaves the final concept of Agent demarcated from other properties of action, but at first unnamed. It exists only by implication of other distinctions having been made. It comes to be explicated, to become a concept he actually *possesses,* when he develops the requisite propositional ability, conceptual knowledge of action, and words to do so. The child has been implicitly referring to agents in speech acts that refer to events occurring through the efforts of others. Through naming these "events" he implicitly creates the concept of an agentive subject, and this concept is finalized—made explicit—through language enabling the possibilities opened up during this development to be actualized.

I find it useful here to turn to Greenfield *et al.*'s original discussion of the emergence of utterances referring to agents (1972: 150–151). They begin with remarks about Matthew's development.

> At the same time as Agents got their first linguistic expression, action words encoding the action of others made their first appearance . . .
>
> The same correlated appearance of the Agent case with words expressing the Action of others held true in Nicky's development too. Another interesting point is the first Agents are not the speaker, a deviation from the development of other cases . . .
>
> There are a number of striking similarities in the development of the Agent case in both children. These help elucidate the question of why Agents remain implicit so long in one-word messages, as is the case for both children.
>
> Remember that both children encoded their own Action before that of others. At this point, we hypothesize, they took themselves for granted as Agents and therefore did not encode self as Agent. For both children there was a close temporal correlation between encoding the Action of others and an ability to express the Agent of anyone's Action in verbal form. Thus, the contrast between one's own action and that of others seemed to lead to an awareness of the very concept of an Agent. This explanation is further supported by the fact that other people were among the first Agents named for both boys, although this differs from what we saw to occur in the development of Object, Action and Negative relations. The close temporal connection between the one- and two-word expression of Agent-Action relations for both children is further evidence in favour of the emergence of Agents in terms of decentration process. Two-word utterances might become desirable when describing the action of others, one no longer takes the Agent for granted and so adds an Agent word to the single word Action message.

The final point concerning the relation between one- and two-word utterances is one I will take up later. Here I wish to note firstly the similarity between this view and the one being developed here, and secondly emphasize the point on which there is a great divergence.

That point is: "remember that both children encoded their own Action before that of others. At this point, we hypothesize, they took themselves for granted as Agents and therefore did not encode self as Agent". The view here is that the child has to *create* himself as an object in his own perceptions if he is to be able to "encode self as agent" just as he has to with "the other". It is only after he comes to perceive another objectively as an agent that this creation is reflected back to himself and he becomes an object to himself. This departure from the usual pattern of decentration is an inevitable one in the context of these present arguments concerning language development in terms of semantic forces and their conjoint natural implicates. While the child may be treated by others as implicitly possessing an ability which later he will manifest explicitly, it would be a mistake to treat him as already "taking it for granted"; to repeat an earlier formulation: a creative process of guided reinvention requiring at every stage the help of others already knowledgeable about the goals to be attained seems to be involved.

What I have been tracing here has been the path by which the child achieves a distinction between an action and its effects by focusing on an object. This results in his creating, reinventing under guidance, the propositional ability necessary for him to then draw a distinction between an agent and the action he performs upon objects—which results in those objects changing their state; and secondly, in his gradually extending this new ability to occasions on which another's actions are directly implied in the situations he is commenting on. He gradually moves on to making this implication explicit, to predicate some change in an objects state to another's action. Through these developments in action and state utterances he moves to a position where he can, through the resulting changes in his perceptions and the development of the propositional ability, refer explicitly to another agent or their actions.

9.2.5 Action-labelling: the emergence of locative and dative utterances

The final development during the one-word stage that I wish to discuss is the emergence of locative and dative utterances. These are again closely related to the above developments occurring in action and state utterances: change in location is a facet of a change in state that results from some action; the experiencer of an action (coded by the dative function) is again very close to the inanimate object of a direct action, differing essentially in being animate.

Greenfield and Smith (1976: 138), discussing Matthew's development, note: "the first example of expression of the Action of an Object in a Volitional context occurred during session IV—16(2), when Matthew went to a closed window and said *down,* asking for the window to be opened". Here, *down* has a very indeterminate status: a request perhaps that another performs a specific action upon the window; or a demand aimed at procuring a desired state for the window; or . . . it might even be a locative. Spatial concomitants of action are obviously ripe candidates for explication by the child from his earliest action-naming abilities. Concerning these aspects Greenfield *et al.* (1972: 143–144) write:

> Both Nicky and Matthew develop the ability to differentiate the Locus of an Action from the Action itself and from the Object of an Action, both in relation to Action of an Agent and Action of an Object, and this differentiation comes relatively late in the one-word stage, long after the concepts of Action and Object have become productive relations. Object Location is by definition a decentred relation in that it involves a relation between two aspects of the world external to the speaker, and this characteristic fits with its relatively late development.

Thus from its definition it may be expected that so-called locative utterances will not appear in an unequivocal form until the child's emerging propositional ability is fully consolidated, i.e. after utterances referring to another's actions, and the objects of his actions become productive. This does appear to be the case for Matthew and Nicky.

Similarly, expectations may be advanced concerning the appearance of utterances classed as instances of the dative case—"the case of the animate being affected by the state or action identified by the verb" (Fillmore, 1968: 24). Without entering into a detailed discussion of the differentiation of transitive and intransitive action, the following may be expected concerning the time at which this case becomes productive, and the nature of its productivity:

(a) probably after that of the Inanimate Object of Direct Action, and probably before that of Action of (non-self) Agent, since the other is passive in the dative role and thus it is not necessary for the child to distinguish Agent and Action, only Action and Object;

(b) the child will label the experience of self-actions prior to the experiencer of the actions of another agent. This latter ability may be

expected to emerge after the child is capable of naming the actions of
that other agent. These expectations are confirmed in Greenfield and
Smith's data (1976: 139–142).

Brown's view that "the first sentences express the construction of
reality which is the terminal achievement of sensori-motor intelligence" (1973: 200) has already been discussed. The above arguments
suggest that his view is incorrect, for it implies as it stands that
language is a function that merely codes concepts that the child has
already developed. Rather it can now be seen to be the case that
language *reconstructs* sensori-motor knowledge and thus effects a transition to objective knowledge. Neither the advent of the proposition nor
the changes it engenders in the child's conception of the world—from
egocentric to exocentric—can be ascribed solely to the terminal
achievements of sensori-motor intelligence as they are generally
thought of. Nor is it the case that the child has to go beyond the
sensori-motor level to greater achievements before he can use propositions, since it is only through the emergence of propositions that he
achieves anything greater. The point I wish to emphasize here is this:
prior to language the child does not possess objective concepts of
reality. To say that the pre-language child can be seen as *possessing* a
concept of agency is different from saying that the post-language child
possesses a concept of agency. A sensori-motor knowledge of agency
differs markedly from the knowledge necessary for its linguistic realization. Language development transforms the child's knowledge in the
same way that a stone thrown into a mill pond transforms it into a
rippling mass: it is the same water, only it has a different form; it is the
same child, but in possession of knowledge in a different form.

9.3 Overview of the one-word stage

On the basis of the above consideration of the emergence of semantic
functions in early child language it is possible to put forward a theoretical sequence for the order of emergence of these functions. This sequence is presented in Table 9.4. The question then arises as to how this
proposed sequence, founded on the concepts of semantic force and their
conjoint natural implicates, squares with recent empirical studies of
this stage of development. Leonard (1975) provides a comprehensive
review of these studies (see especially his Chapters 1 and 5), and rather

Table 9.4. A tentative outline of the emergence of single-word uses.

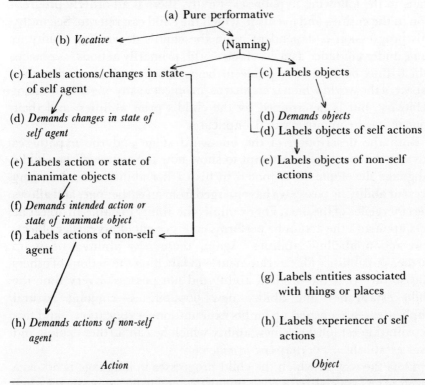

Italicized entries in the table indicate occasions the relevant word is used in combination with a gesture.

than my discussing all these studies here the reader is referred to that review. The evidence gives broad support to this scheme provided two related points are kept in mind. The first of these is that because of the high indeterminacy of meaning in single-word speech it is practically impossible to talk of the point at which any function *actually* emerges (for a related discussion see Lock, 1976), or even to classify reliably an utterance as an instance of one particular semantic notion rather than another. Secondly, there is the question of whether or not any semantic notion that might unequivocally be delineated in a child's speech on one occasion indicates that notion to be so well established as to be regarded as productive. As the proverb goes, one swallow does not make a summer. But if both of these problems are recognized, then this scheme appears to hold.

This survey of the development of single word utterances by the child leads to the following hypotheses. Firstly, there is an orderly progression in the entities and events to which the child can refer to. Secondly, this progression is dependent upon the child's developing ability to *create* under guidance aspects of the world, primarily actions, as objects which thus become susceptible to being labelled. And thirdly, that aspect of the world which is created as an object at any one instant is not arbitrary, but is determined by the child's prior abilities, and their concomitant conjoint natural implicates.

Both the description of the one-word stage and the hypotheses advanced above are an attempt to show how the course of the child's language development is rooted in his earlier abilities, i.e. how any present ability he possesses has emerged from an earlier one, and allows the emergence of the next. For example, the ability to name an object he acts upon and the action he performs emerges out of his earlier object- and action-labelling abilities. Again, these new abilities open up further possibilities for development—to labelling the actions of others and so on—that the original ability did not possess. Every time the child establishes one ability new possibilities—conjoint natural implicates—are opened up for his exploitation—explication—and this exploitation establishes a new ability which he can further exploit and thus establish . . . perhaps *ad infinitum*.

Thus the way in which the child progresses in language is not as a result of any specialized *a priori* linguistic knowledge he possesses, such as an innate conception of a sentence, but in a way commensurate with more general properties he possesses as an infant embedded in a society. What happens in his development of language is of the same nature as the processes operating in the development of his other abilities (see also below on the appearance of two-word speech). Obviously if one of the earliest functions of child speech were the naming of agents other than himself it would be necessary to invoke innate linguistic knowledge as an explanatory concept. For since such an ability would essentially "appear from nowhere", the child having no basis in his previous abilities for making such an utterance, there would be no other way of accounting for the appearance of this function in his repertoire. But since this does not happen this course need not be taken.

To these three hypotheses a fourth may be added: that before a word may be used within a demand function it must be used previously in a labelling one. This insertion of words into demand structures may aid in the creation of new objects susceptible to naming. For example, the child is capable of naming his performances, and then of requesting that performance—he is able to say *down* while going down prior to asking to go down. In using *down* in a demand he implicates the mother's performance in the execution of his intentions, and the actions she must perform in realizing this intention have effectively become the focus of the child's attention. His word and her action thus doubtless become "associated" so that those actions gain assistance in their objectification by the child as equivalent to what is already being named by that word. The reference of *down* is then creatively extended through its implications by use to the actions of another in addition to the actions or experiences of the child.

It is apparent that there are many pitfalls, some unavoidable, when it comes to the task of assigning an interpretation to the child's early word use, or to classifying them under one semantic notion or another. This is the main reason for having adopted Sanborn's position (1971) as one of the basic tenets of this study. To reiterate his position: the development of language may be looked at from the "genitico-historical standpoint with adult speech as the end development". Returning to Matthew's utterance *cold* (see Section 9.2.3) the usefulness of this view can be seen. It was suggested that this utterance did not refer to the *air* Matthew was feeling, but to his *experience* of actually feeling it: but this interpretation is only more acceptable on the grounds of parsimony, and cannot be empirically substantiated.

The interpretations given to these early utterances by those who deal with the child, however, are made from the adult standpoint—as is the interpretation put forward by Greenfield *et al.* (1972) in this case. And if, as Ryan maintains,

> the context of rich interpretation provided by many mothers, combined with the considerable ambiguity of many one-word utterances, provides an extremely informative situation for the child as regards what she is taken to be meaning   (1974: 205)

then the essence of the interactive process is that of "homing" the child in on the adult meaning; of helping him hit the target. *Cold* is treated as referring to that state of an object when in fact it probably refers to the experience of feeling "cold". And as has been argued, treating some action "as if it means such and such" is a very powerful technique. Whatever the utterance might actually refer to is essentially irrelevant: the perceived referent is the important factor.

To this instance of *cold* may be added the case of *down*. *Down* has many potential uses and meanings, and all these are subsumed in its early occurrences: to begin with it is truly indeterminate—but not indeterminable. While arguments have been advanced here as to why *down* should be considered to be at first totally tied up with the child's bodily experiences, its early uses implicate all manner of adult conceptions. When Nicky says *down* as he pulls his train down (Greenfield and Smith, 1976: 131) at 18 (27) the utterance could refer to: (a) Nicky's experience of moving his arm; (b) the movement of the object; (c) its resultant change in state; or (d) the locus or spatial end-point of his action. These are its potential meanings, but they are not yet made explicit by the child, they are only implicit in what he says. They can only be realized through the process of interaction.

That the child comes to use words in the cases of state, action, agent and so on cannot be accounted for by postulating his innate possession of such concepts, as Fillmore suggests:

> [They] comprise a set of universal, presumably innate, concepts which identify certain types of judgments human beings are capable of making about the events that are going on around them, judgments about such matters as who did it, who it happened to, and what got changed.
>
> (1968: 24)

What the child *must* be innately capable of is creating these concepts, but the exact concepts are created by negotiation between him and his culture. We only see the early stirrings of concepts such as agent in the child's early language, pre-language behaviour and actions in his social world because we possess that concept ourselves: it is not really there, only potentially there. And it follows that it need never actually be realized, just as Eskimos never realize the concept of "being".

Carpenter's description of Eskimo art and the way it is created also capture entirely this phase in the child's development (1966: 206):

> Art to the Eskimo is far more than an object: it is a ritual of exploration by which patterns of nature, and of human nature, are revealed by man.
>
>   As the carver holds the unworked ivory lightly in his hand, turning it this way and that, he whispers, "Who are you? Who hides there?" And then: "Ah, Seal!" He rarely sets out to carve, say, a seal, but picks up the ivory, examines it to find its hidden form and, if that is not immediately apparent, carves aimlessly until he sees it, humming or chanting as he works. Then he brings it out: seal, hidden, emerges. It was always there: he did not create it. He released it: he helped it step forth.

The forms an Eskimo finds hidden in his material are culturally determined: he will find whales and fish and polar-bears, not lions or tigers or even motor-cars. Then he works to reveal those forms that are already there. And this is exactly how mothers should be conceived, as working to reveal what is already there in their children. What they see as already there is a cultural interpretation, concepts which have their origins somewhere in their culture's past, and not in the innate nature of their offspring.

What infants do is to *create spontaneously* new situations and contexts in which they can use a word. The child draws out for himself the implications of his previous abilities, using the symbolic language functions he already possesses as tools. It is doubtful that he is taught to extend his word usage, unlikely that he learns by acquiring external information how to label an object he is acting on. Doubtful and unlikely because firstly his mother does not appear to teach him, at least not by the same method as she taught him words in the first place; and secondly, that before he names an object he is acting on he cannot conceive the situation in a way that would enable him to use the object word: he would have to learn something he could not conceive. The impetus thus seems to come from within: the child deduces the concept from his earlier "concepts", which "imply" what he "deduces". This is not to maintain that the mother has no role at this time, she must act as his guide.

This ability of the child's to *create spontaneously* new ways of conceiving and perceiving situations is an ability that may also be characterized by saying that he is able to *discover* spontaneously and creatively that way of conception, since that way was opened up as a possibility by his earlier attainments with their *conjoint natural implicates*.

The question which prompted this consideration of the one-word period of language development was: Why does the verbalization of the Objects of Actions performed by an agent other than the child lag behind the verbalization of the Objects of his own Actions? The answer that stems from this consideration is that to name the objects of another's acts requires a more advanced knowledge than the achievements of the sensori-motor stage allow. This is not the case for objects of one's own actions, and this ability is itself a step in the inevitable transition to objective knowledge. Until that knowledge is created, propositions cannot be uttered: but paradoxically, that knowledge is only created through the uttering of propositions. This paradox can only be resolved by considering the development of language and knowledge as inextricably entwined during this time in the child's life; and by remembering that in developmental processes no activity or ability has a definite "birthday". To borrow a phrase from recent advance in mathematical theory, the relationship between our linguistic concepts and the "objects" they refer to is "fuzzy".

10. Two-word utterances

This chapter considers the development of multi-word utterances, again based on the data corpus of Greenfield's study (Greenfield *et al.*, 1972; Greenfield and Smith, 1976). Separating these utterances from single-word ones unfortunately gives the impression that the two stages are distinct. This is not the case: some classes of one-word utterances, for example, those referring to agents, make their appearance *after* the child has become capable of using two-word utterances. The two stages thus overlap, and in some instances they interact. It is probably no longer useful to think of the child's linguistic development in terms of stages delineated from each other by mean utterance length, and so on: in terms of concepts which have a purely linguistic reference. These two periods, of one- and multi-word utterances, have been kept separate, then, purely as a matter of convenience.

10.1 Two-word utterances

10.1.1 Single words, sequences and two words

In surveying their data Greenfield *et al.* (1972, 1976) find that the transition from one- to two-word speech occurs not directly, but with an intervening period in which the child produces two one-word utterances sequentially, with a gap of $1 \cdot 1 - 4 \cdot 0$ seconds separating each word. And as they point out,

G

a number of earlier observers of child speech (e.g., Guillaume, 1927; Stern, 1930; Leopold, 1949; Cohen, 1952) have noticed the occurence of sequences of single-word utterances as a later stage within one-word speech.   (Greenfield and Smith, 1976: 41)

Table 10.1. Instances of two-word utterances (see text).

Preceding context	Modality			Event
(a) *Matthew* V, 17 (13)				
1. Vocative				
	M	wh, r trying to get *mommy*		whistle
2. Object of demand				
	M	wh pointing to bananas *nana*		
3. Action of agent in high chair	wh, r		M	trying to get *down*
4. Vocative-action sequence in high chair	M	wh, r *mommy*		*down*
5. Vocative-demand sequence				
	M	reaching for piggy bank *mommy*		
What?				*bappy* (bank)
(b) *Matthew* VI, 19 (21)				
6. Vocative-action two-word utterance				
M gives medicine to mother.	M	*mommy*		*up* (open)

Note: wh = whining; r = reaching

Immediately a parallel between this development and that which occurred much earlier in the case of gestures suggests itself. This parallel can be seen more clearly by considering Matthew's utterances listed in Table 10.1, and this leads to the view that developmentally the *sentences* of the child's emerging language may be *internalized acts*.

Table 10.1. presents utterances from Matthew's corpus as reported by Greenfield *et al.* (1976). Utterances 1–5 occurred during observation session V—17(13), and utterance 6 during session VII—19(21). In the same way that structures could be ascribed to gestural acts, they can also be ascribed to speech acts. Structures for utterances 1–3 have already been discussed (above Sections 9.4.2 and 9.4.4); they may be given as in Fig. 10.1. All three structures are concerned with utterances possessing a demand connotation, and they reflect again the inter-

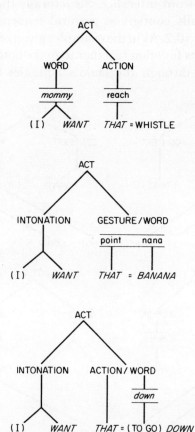

Fig. 10.1. Act-structures for utterances 1-3, Table 10.1.

dependence of early communicative speech acts and previous gestural strategies. In 1 (Table 10.1), the word used by Matthew functions to make a relationship determinate; in 2 and 3 they function to determine the object Matthew is placing himself in relation to. In all three cases the portion of the communicative act that is not made totally explicit by the child's utterance is capable of being made so within a different act: i.e. what is implicit in 1 is made explicit in 2 and 3; and what is implicit in 2 and 3 is made explicit in 1. The structural aspects of Matthew's word usage at this stage in his development thus parallels that found in the earlier stages of communication noted above for Peter, Paul and Mary.

This parallel is extended in the cases of 4 and 5 above in which two words are used in sequence—i.e. as two proximal one-word utterances and not as one two-word utterance. Structurally these utterances are akin to the temporally contiguous gestural sequencing noted earlier (Chapter 6); see Fig. 10.2. As in the examples given of gestural sequencing, two separate acts function together to make both relationship and object determinate through the child's activities alone. What was

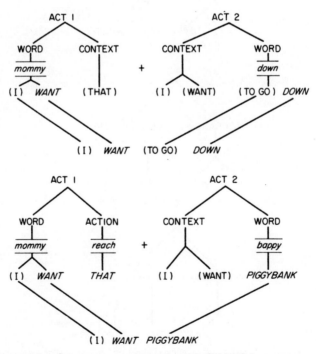

Fig. 10.2. Act-structures for utterance sequences 4 and 5, Table 10.1.

previously left to contextual determination in Act 1 is now made determinate in Act 2—and the contextual dependency of Act 2 is replaced by the word used in Act 1.

The ultimate appearance of two-word utterances may thus be accounted for by the same process operating in the gestural period by the coalescence of the separate acts to yield a single two-word act, for example utterance 6 (Fig. 10.3).

The apparent emphasis here upon gestural structures, word – gesture substitution and subsequent coalescence is *not* intended to suggest that the structure or grammar of the child's emerging spoken language arises merely as a result of the child substituting words for gestures in previously developed structures or schemes. Word–gesture substitution is certainly important in the development of language, and some two-word combinations do have their origins in previously developed gestural structures: but equally not all two-word utterances have such a basis. The intention is rather to show that the processes *underlying* the child's ability to combine his gestures is the same process as that responsible for his being able to combine his words; and that similarly the roots of grammar go back beyond the two-word period.

One continuing argument in developmental psycholinguistics has been the structural status of the one-word period. This argument revolves around the position that the concept of the sentence plays in differing theoretical approaches to language development. There is little dispute that two-word utterances have a "sentence-structure", but this is not the case where one-word utterances are concerned (see for example, Bloom 1973; Ingram, 1971; McNeill, 1970). But if we take the view that a sentence is an act whose structure has been "internalized" this argument can be resolved. One-word utterances have no

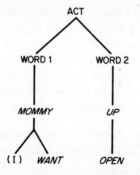

Fig. 10.3. Act-structure of two-word utterance 6 in Table 10.1.

sentential structure, but they occur within structured acts. In other words, one-word utterances *are structured*, but the word is only a part of a greater structure, the act in which it is produced. In this context the developmental history of two-word utterances that arise directly from the earlier use of a gesture and a word provides a clear example of the fact that from the age of a year the child's *communicative* abilities are structured, and that the one- and two-word stages only differ in *the form* in which that structure is realized.

This combinatorial process operates, then, both prior to and during language emergence, and there is consequently no need to invoke innate grammars to account for the development of early language structures. The child is not *given* structures for the production of patterned speech—at least in its early stages—but he *creates* those structures: he does not *learn* how to produce such speech, he *invents* ways of producing it. Any structure is initially to be found implicitly in the child's *spontaneous* transactions with the world, and only later *explicitly* in his *deliberate* transactions. We may view "language" as internalized acting in the same way as Piaget views thought as internalized action.

In this context it is illuminating to note Gruber's discussion (1967) of the development of the topic–comment syntactic structure, reported by him as being used by one child in contradistinction to the normal subject–predicate construction of English—his parents' language—at the age of a little over two years. What is illuminating here is that the child in question had no opportunity to learn this form of construction. In English, an example of this form of construction would be, to use Gruber's example (1967: 37), " 'Salt, I taste it in this food', 'salt' is the topic, and 'I taste it in this food', is the comment."

> While such constructions as these seem somewhat accessory to the adult grammar of English, they were essential to the child's grammar at the stage under study. Moreover, this type of construction was absent in our data for the speech of the child's exclusively English speaking parents. The child could thus have had no model for these constructions and they must therefore represent independent creations of his own (based perhaps on creative interpretations of adult speech). (Gruber, 1967:38)

Interestingly, such topic–comment constructions form an essential part of the grammars of adult Chinese and Japanese, as well as many other non-European languages.

Now prior to the period of two-word usage, a child possesses a demand structure comprising a word and gesture, a structure classified by Greenfield *et al.* (1972) under the heading of "Object of Demand", which may be given as shown in Fig. 10.4. But as already noted, the word/gesture structures of the child at this stage possess no inherent time patterning—the word and gesture being produced simultaneously—and thus it becomes impossible to choose between the structure just given and its possible alternative, shown in Fig. 10.5. The further development of each of these structures in the manner that has been described will yield in patterned speech *either* a subject–predicate *or* a topic–comment structure. Rather than relating such structures in two-word speech to "creative interpretations of adult speech" as Gruber suggests, they may again be related to the child himself: they are his own creations and as such do not bear any relation to the structure of the language used in his environment.

Again a *communicative* structure has been used in illustrating these creative processes, but it can be shown that two-word propositional or referential utterances also have a similar developmental history. That

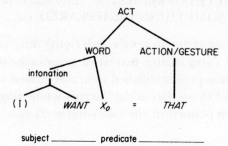

Fig. 10.4. Possible act-structure for single-word "object of demand" utterance, having subject–predicate form.

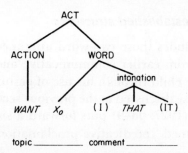

Fig. 10.5. Alternative act-structure for single-word "object of demand" utterance, having topic–comment form.

they arise in this way has been hinted at by Bloom (1973), and with this current background her comments can be expanded. Her study of her own daughter, Allison, lead her to the view that:

> Linguistically, the potential juxtaposition of . . . "certain words" . . . with other "words" could generally be predicted from the context in which they occurred. When Allison said "more" as she reached for another cookie, it was not difficult to predict the connection between the words "more" and "cookie"; and, indeed, utterances like "more cookie" occurred from time to time. When such two-word utterances as "more cookie" occurred . . . the nature of the relation between the two-words derived from the relational nature of the word with constant form and consistent use in each repeated situation (cf. existence, non-existence, recurrence, etc.). That is, the meaning of the relationships between the words was dependent upon the meaning of one of the words—for example, "more", "no", "up", or "a'gone". It was concluded that Allison's early sporadic two-word utterances were not manifestations of any underlying rule-system but, rather, were a manifestation of the essentially transitive nature of the notions coded by the particular forms "more", "away", "stop", etc., to the nonlinguistic states of affairs to which they referred. SOMETHING had to STOP; there had to be SOMETHING TO RECUR; SOMETHING DISAPPEARED, etc.   (1973: 114)

To elucidate some of the processes underlying this "potential juxtaposition" requires categorizing two-word utterances into three classes: those derived from pre-established structures; those that occur "within predicates"; and those that occur "across whole propositions". These categories are explained in the following section.

10.1.2 Categories of two-word utterances and their establishment

(a) Via pre-established structures

This category includes those two-word utterances whose structure is directly derived from earlier communicative and referential abilities established by the child through his use of gesture. Examples of such utterances are those discussed in the previous section: *mommy down; this* (X_o). De Laguna (1927: 98–9) puts forward a similar view in discussing what she termed "predicative proclamation":

> What is proclaimed in (predicative proclamation) always has reference to some object or event or general state of affairs whose existence is *presumed*.

This presumption may take the form of pointing to the thing in question, or perhaps of intently regarding it. The predicative proclamation does not announce its presence or existence, but calls attention to some specific property having a bearing on the given situation. In such a case there is virtual or implicit predication; but the language form is rudimentary. The verbal utterance must be supplemented by some other form of bodily response, like pointing, which serves to indicate the object to which the verbal specification applies .... What is needed to transform this rudimentary predication into the full-fledged sentence, is that the act of pointing or otherwise indicating the object be replaced by an act of speech, the utterance of a word.

Two-word utterances in the next two categories arise from the sequencing of two one-word utterances, these then coalescing to yield a two-word act. Later emerging "cases" enter into two-word acts immediately, suggesting that earlier coalescences lead to a general combinatory ability.

(b) *Within "predicates"*

Instances of utterances in this category are: Bloom's example, noted immediately above, of *more cookie*; from Greenfield *et al.* (1972) Matthew making a demand—*more cookie*; Matthew holding his hat—*my hat*; Matthew in response to the question "Where has ice gone"—*gone bye bye*. In these examples the two-word utterance occurs as part of the "predicate" of the semantic force of the communicative/referential speech act, i.e.

(a) (I) (WANT) *MORE COOKIE*
(b) (THAT) (IS) *MY HAT*/(I) (AM HOLDING) *MY HAT*
(c) (ICE) (IS?) *GONE BYEBYE*

Sequences of this type also occur, both within dialogues and without: for example, Matthew in session V—17(13) has had spagettioes to eat. He holds out his empty plate and says *more*. This prompts the question "Do you want more spagettioes?" to which he "replies" *ettios*.

The establishment of such two-word utterances does not present any conceptual problem to the child, and along with those in (a) above should be the earliest form of two-word utterance to be found in the child's repertoire. Doubtless they will be more common than the former, since they have an inherently greater potential productivity. Their occurrence is, as Bloom notes, "not difficult to predict", and their production is not entangled with problems concerning the child's development of the ability to make the subjects of his semantic forces explicit, to make propositions, as is the case in the next category.

That this form of two-word utterance precedes those in the next category is confirmed by the data corpus of Greenfield *et al.* Further support comes from Leonard's (1976) re-analysis of Braine's (1976) longitudinal data for two children, Jonathan and David. For the first sample from Jonathan, Leonard (1976: 33) notes the following notions (examples given in brackets):

> Nonexistence (*all gone stick*)
> Recurrence (*more book*)
> Action (*eat grape*)
> Object (*eat grape*)
> Possessor (*Daddy pipe*)
> Attribution (*little key*)
> Experience (*hurt toe*)

In the second, sample, several new notions emerged.

> Agent (*Andrew walk*)
> Experiencer (*hurt Andrew*)
> Instrument (*eat fork*)
> Classificatory (*Mommy girl*)
> Comitative (*walk Daddy*)
> Conjunction (*sock shoe*) . . . .

In the first sample from David, I observed evidence of following semantic notions.

> Nomination (*this one here*)
> Notice (*here milk*)
> Recurrence (*more balloon*)
> Action (*fix it*)
> Object (*fix it*)

Several new notions emerged in David's second sample.

> Agent (*Daddy sit*)
> Attribution (*good boy*)
> Possessor (*Baby toy*)
> Experience (*like it*)
> Experiencer (*baby cry*)
> Completion (*all finish that*)

In both cases it is apparent that two-word utterances of the "within predicate" variety occur before those of the "cross proposition" form.

(c) *Across entire propositions*

Once the child has established the ability to use semantic forces of a propositional nature, and can linguistically realize elements from both their subjects and predicates, a new class of two-word utterances becomes possible: utterances in which both subject and object, or topic and comment, are verbalized. Their appearance, then, requires a conceptual development, and they are likely to be the last form of two-word utterance to appear.

In a longitudinal study of seven children at this period in their language development, Ramer (1974) found four of the children to be rapid in their development of new syntactic classes, and three to be much slower. Leonard (1976: 42) notes that:

> the rapid developers specified the three grammatical relations of subject and verb, subject and complement, and verb and complement at the onset of syntax. The slow developers began by specifying only the verb and complement of the three.

Leonard (1976: 43) goes on to observe that:

> Werner and Kaplan (1963) identified two types of early word combinations, one where the expression of the word combination could be likened to a single-word expression since the individual element overlaps too extensively to form a true grammatical relationship, perhaps resembling functional relations, and the other representing word combinations where the two elements of the utterance emphasise different features of the presented event and approach a sentential relationship. Such word combinations seem to resemble what Bloom (1973) termed grammatical relations. Consistent within the observations of Brown (1973), Werner and Kaplan pointed out that the former types of utterances seem to appear before the latter.

Both these points tie in with the suggestion that conceptual development is necessarily related to the appearance of this category of two-word speech. Once that development has occurred, however, the processes by which word sequences of this latter category are generated operate as soon as the conceptual development is evidenced in word use. If this class of utterance were distinct, then even though the child is already sequencing words *before* "subject" words appear, an appreciable lag might be expected before two-word sequences of the nature subject–object occur. But this is not the case: certainly for Matthew there is a slight delay, but in Nicky's case sequencing of these elements occurs immediately, and thus two-word utterances may form by coalescence. Therefore, the ability to put words into a sequence is a general ability which can be extended to apply to propositional utterances following its development with non-propositional ones.

Further, the ability to combine words is a general one. Proper two-word utterances occur before some semantic cases make their appearance even as single words. Yet in discussing two such late emerging cases—Agent of Action and Action of non-self Agent—Greenfield *et al.* (1972: 113) note:

> two-word Agent-Action utterances occur [for both Matthew and Nicky], as soon as the Action of *other* Agents becomes a productive relation. Agent-Action sequences are non-existent in Nicky's corpus, rare in Matthew's.

The combinatory ability is, then, a general one. These developments further emphasize that the child's exposure to the grammatical language of his environment is not of crucial importance for his developing patterned speech.

From the discussion, I think that firstly it is no longer productive to view the child as passing through distinct stages delineated as preverbal, one-word and two-word. Pre-propositional and post-propositional may suffice should a need for categorization prevail, but it is perhaps more important to remember the interrelatedness of these early developments rather than any apparent dissimilarities they may exhibit. Secondly, a point about grammar: grammar can be found within the child's language, but not within the child. From the structural point of view there is little need—up to the two-word stage—to look for an innate language acquisition device. From the semantic viewpoint, the semantic cases which emerge do so as the result of an interaction between the child's natural power to make sense of his perception of the world—to create meaningful objects within it—and the social world which provides both the substrate and the environment in which perception is structured and made meaningful.

11. Self-reflection and self-creation

Present day psychologists are used to thinking of cognitive and social psychology as two separate areas of concern within the subject. In Mead's approach to the development of the self, however, this distinction is not made. For example, he considers (1934: 173) that:

> The essence of the self . . . is cognitive: it lies in the internalised conversation of gestures which constitute thinking, or in terms of which thought or reflection proceeds. And hence the origin and foundations of the self, like those of thinking, are social.

It will be apparent that the position Mead takes is paralleled by that of Vygotsky—that functions exist on the intermental (social) level before they exist on the intramental (cognitive) level. Mead in fact gives his own separate formulation of Vygotsky's (1966) proposed law of cultural development (1934: 172):

> The self and self-consciousness have first to arise, and then these experiences can be identified peculiarly with the self, or appropriated by the self; to enter, so to speak, into this heritage of experience, the self has first to develop within the social process in which this heritage is involved.

This conception of the development of the self may be grasped through the idea of "fictitious imagery". As was noted in discussing the contextual aspects of communicative development in Chapter 4, the mother has a "cultural image" of her infant. She perceives her child anthropomorphically, as if he were already a human being. Thus if the child holds out an object towards her, she interprets this action as the child intending to give her the object, and she does this well before the child is in fact capable of giving objects. It is, then, useful to think of the mother–child dyad as a triad: not composed of two individuals, but of three; the mother, her child, and *between* them the mother's image of the child. For the purpose of this "fictitious imagery" theory I propose that this image is thought of as a physical thing actually present between the mother and child during their interactions. Now this image is not static. It does not have constant "physical characteristics" from the day the child is born. Rather, it changes. As the mother gains knowledge of her particular child, her image of the child changes. This process was again discussed in Chapter 4: her image of the child becomes comprised not only of what she intends her child to be, but also what she knows he is—a child who picks up small pieces of fluff, for example. Thus, as the child grows, the mother's image of him also grows. This is the social aspect of the development of the self. Through social interaction the initial image develops into the image of the particular child, and this image is the child's self.

Considering the cognitive side of the process, the fact that the fictitious image is located only in the mother becomes important. While the "dyad" consists of three individuals, only the mother can see this physical thing termed her imagined child: only she can see his self. The infant, to begin with, is *blind* with respect to it. Cooley (1902) put forward the notion of the "looking-glass self": that the mother acts as a mirror, reflecting the child back to himself. Here I am suggesting more of a "one-way" or "dirty-mirror" notion: that the child's reflection is somehow trapped in the mirror, not immediately reflected back by it. Cognitive development is then the process by which the child acquires a duster, and thereby cleans the mirror so that he can see the "reflection" that his mother can already see—"taking . . . the attitude of the other toward yourself is what constitutes self-consciousness" (Mead, 1934: 171). The self, then, is constituted as a social object, and initially it exists beyond the child's comprehension. It is through his internalizing social gestures to constitute his thoughts that the child becomes able to grasp and comprehend this social object for himself.

This grasping and coming to comprehend is the process I have been discussing in earlier chapters in terms of giving explicit form to those "things" which are implied by the infant's existence and actions. Through the guided reinvention of language the child comes to share in his culture's explicit perception of the world. Initially his words are tied up with his actions and experiences, but gradually he progresses to use them objectively. To begin with he uses "action words" such as *up* only when he is in motion—when he is the actor, the action, and the object of the action. Performing or experiencing such an action necessitates implicitly a change in physical position, attention.

Not only is the child now in the throes of distinguishing actors from their actions, actions from their effects and objects from the actions they undergo, he is concurrently establishing knowledge of these "entities" independently of himself. Knowledge of places in relation to objects which are not him; of objects in relation to actions which are not his; and so on. And he begins to know *himself* from this independent perspective. Others are differentiated from their actions, their actions are seen as equivalent to his own. He comes to see himself from the perspective of others: by this tortuous route the child wipes the mirror clean and thereby gains that perspective upon himself which we term self-awareness.

It is important to remember at this point that the child sees himself in relation to the way others see the world. Remember also that it is through language that the world is given its form. Carpenter (1966: 208) points out, in discussing Eskimo language, that

> Language is the principle tool with which the Eskimos make the natural world a human world. They use many "words" for snow which permit fine distinctions, not simply because they are much concerned with snow, but because snow takes its form from the actions in which it participates: sledding, falling, igloo-building, blowing. These distinctions are possible only when experienced in a meaningful context. Different kinds of snow are brought into existence by the Eskimos as they experience their environment and speak; the words do not label something already there. Words, for the Eskimo, are like the knife of the carver: they free the idea, the thing, from the general formlessness of the outside.

Words make explicit what previously exists only implicitly. But many different things are implied by our actions in the world: they may be given many different explicit forms of characterization; for example, "what we call action, Eskimos see and describe as a pattern of succeding impressions" (Carpenter, 1966: 218). Again, in English we make a distinction between nouns and verbs, yet sometimes we are not sure how we ought to apply these words to an event: "it rained yesterday" or "rain fell yesterday" are quite different conceptions. By contrast, Eskimos make little distinction between nouns and verbs, "rather all

words are forms of the verb 'to be', which is itself lacking in Eskimo''
(Carpenter, 1966: 206). Similarly, there are some "important events"
that we do not make explicit. As Collingwood sees it, "some 'events' of
interest to the historian are not actions but the opposite, for which we
have no English word: not *actions* but *passiones*, instances of being acted
upon" (1939: 128 fn). Again, Lee (1950: 91) in her classic re-analysis of
Malinowski's field data from the Trobriand Isles, notes that

> What we consider an attribute of a predicate, is to the Trobriander an
> ingredient. Where I would say, for example, "A good gardener," or "The
> gardener is good", the Trobriand word would include both "gardener"
> and "goodness"; if the gardener loses the goodness he has lost a defining
> ingredient, he is something else, and is named by means of a completely
> different word. A *taytu* (a species of yam) contains a certain degree of
> ripeness, bigness, roundedness, etc.; without one of these defining ingre-
> dients, it is something else, perhaps a *bwanawa* or a *yowana*. There are no
> adjectives in the language; the rare words dealing with qualities are
> substantivized. The term *to be* does not occur; it is used neither attribu-
> tively nor existentially, since existence itself is contained; it is an ingre-
> dient of being.

There are, thus, many linguistic realities for infants to be guided into;
and consequently many potential conceptions of self. For example, in
discussing the difficult question of differences between Dinka (a tribe of
the Southern Sudan) and European self-knowledge, Lienhardt (1961:
149) argues that:

> The Dinka have no conception that at all corresponds to our popular
> conception of the "mind" as mediating and . . . storing up the experiences
> of the self. There is for them no such interior entity to appear, on reflection
> to stand between the experiencing self at any given moment and what is or
> has been an exterior influence upon the self. . . . So it seems that what we
> should call in some cases the "memories" of experiences, and regard
> therefore as . . . intrinsic and interior to the remembering person . . .
> appear to the Dinka as exteriorly acting upon him.

What we might term "memories" are conceived by the Dinka as
external *Powers*, "as living agents influencing their lives for good or
evil" (1961: 147):

> It is perhaps significant that in ordinary English usage we have no word
> to indicate an opposite of "actions" in relation to the human self. If the
> word "passions", *passiones*, were still normally current as the opposite of
> "actions", it would be possible to say that the Dinka Power were the

images of human *passiones* seen as the active sources of those *passiones*. (1961: 151)

It would further be possible to say that the Dinka image of self is remarkably different from the one we possess. Similarly, as may be expected,

> The Eskimo view of self is not as clearly demarcated as ours, and its precise limits often vary according to circumstances. They do not reduce the self to a sharply delimited, consistent, controlling "I". (Indeed, the Eskimo language contains no first-person pronoun, which in English is so important we make "I" upper case, an honour otherwise restricted to gods and kings). They postulate no personality "structure", but accept the clotted nature of experience—the simultaneity of good and evil, of joy and despair, multiple models within the one, contraries inextricably comingled. (Carpenter, 1966: 224)

There is no "true" self there for the infant to discover, only one of indeterminately many for him to delineate and reinvent with guidance. Our conception of our selves depends upon our conception of actions, and there are many possible explicit forms for this conception to take. In sum, differing social realities imply different conceptions of self. But one commonality may be hypothesized as holding across all cultures: that the explication of the "self" as an "objective entity" will come at the end of the developmental period in which the referential ability emerges. The "I" can only behold itself from the perspective of the other, and that is a perspective that is not *given* to any one of us: it is one which is attained through the social guidance of cognitive development.

This work has attempted to shed light on how the child's "cognitive" development is guided by the social world in which he lives. It has done this by considering two phases in the development of language: the development of communication and sensori-motor knowledge; and the development of reference, early language use, and objective knowledge. The essential points of these phases are summarized below.

(a) *The development of communication and sensori-motor knowledge*
Communication and sensori-motor knowledge develop hand-in-hand, for while at birth the child is capable of communicating—more precisely he is *perceived* to communicate—he does so naturally and without knowledge. He is, however, innately endowed with criteria—his bodily needs—by which to judge the consequences of his own actions in the

world. Through the possession of these criteria he is able to come to a sensori-motor knowledge of the relation between his actions and certain objects in the world. His possession of this knowledge is reflected in the way he comes to use his actions. These firstly take on an intentional character, but still remain only fortuitously communicative. Next the child "realizes" the communicative function of these actions—that they effect his intentions indirectly through the mediation of another. He begins to "aim" his actions, now termed "gestures", at that other, to make "informed requests" of him or her. Thus through being treated "as if" he could communicate he becomes able to actually do so.

At this time gestures are employed singly; further, their meanings are highly context-dependent: they do not convey "complete" messages, only portions of messages. They function to make determinate *either* the child's need *or* the object implicated by that need. The rest of the message is "decoded" by the listener by reference to contextual factors. Following this stage the child progresses to using his gestures in combination, communicating *both* his need *and* its object. Finally, after the emergence of spoken language, words themselves are used in the pursuit of intentions, in combination with the previously established gestures. Development to this point thus occurs through an interplay between the completion of the child's actions by a social agent, his innate capacity to judge the egocentric value of that conception, and his ability to capitalize upon that judgement.

(a) *The development of language and objective knowledge*

The early stages of language development have two facets. The first is the use of words within the framework of the child's previously developed communicative ability: he begins to employ words where he previously used gestures. The second is his creative exploitation of the inherent referential function of words. This exploitation effects the child's transition from the realm of sensori-motor knowledge to that of objective knowledge. Thus where the first facet represents the translation of an already possessed ability into a linguistic form the second does not. The child does not possess objective concepts in the prelinguistic stage which merely await upon the emergence of language for their expression. He has to exploit the inherent possibilities of his primitive referential ability to create such concepts. This process has been characterized here as the child making explicit the implications of his utterances, and thus using language as a tool to pull himself up by his own bootstraps from egocentric to objective knowledge.

Again, social guidance from adults is involved in this phase of development. But the arguments presented here suggest that if the following experiment, reported by Lindsay of Pitscottie in his *History of Scotland* as occurring in the reign of James IV, were repeated it may well have a different outcome!

> And also the King gart tak one dum woman and put hir in Inchekeytht and gait hir tua zoung bairnes in companie witht hir and gart furnische them of all necessar thing is pertening to thair nurischment that is to say, meit, drink, fire, and candell, claithis, witht all wther kind of necessaris guhilk is reguyrit to man or woman desyrand the effect heirof to come to know guhat language thir bairnes wold speik guhene they come to lauch-full aige. Sum sayis they spak goode hebrew bot as to my self I know not bot the authons reherse. Thir actis foirsaid was done in the zeir of God I^m iiij^c Ixxxxiij zeivis.

It may now be suspected that these bairnes may well go on to invent some form of language in the absence of an external input (see also Goldin-Meadow and Feldman, 1977; Feldman *et al.*, 1978). Language is essentially invented, but usually it is reinvented with social guidance. Both the evolution and development of language can be dealt with from this approach.

While it is useful to deal separately with these two phases of language development—the implicit and the explicit—it is important to remember that they are closely interrelated. Language is "imported" into situations which have already become socially intelligible to the child. Two factors in particular cut across both phases:

(1) *Structure*
The processes operating in both the gestural and verbal stages appear to bear a close relationship to each other. The sequence of gestural development may be summed up as one gesture at a time, then two gestures in sequence, and finally two gestures at a time. In this last stage the child is able to convey a message to his mother through the combination of these different actions. Where previously the message relied heavily upon contextual completion for its meaning it now does not: it is inherently more explicit. Similarly with language: the sequence of development is one word at a time, then two words in a sequence, and finally two words at a time. In the last stage the message is conveyed in the form of a sentence—a structured combination of different actions. One-word utterances are highly context dependent for their communicative power: two-word utterances are necessarily

less so. The cognitive operations which underlie these structured actions arise from the internalization of earlier communicative acts. What is implicit in these is made continually more explicit as development proceeds.

(2) *Implication*

Both phases of development may be characterized through the concept of implication. Dreyfus (1967) has pointed out that a creative discovery is one in which we find out what it was that we wanted all along. Before that discovery occurs its importance or value already implicitly exists in relation to the need. Action results in this implicit value becoming explicitly known, and thus knowledge, purpose and gestures with shared meanings all arise.

Similarly, with language: a single word said while the child is performing an action, being context-dependent for its meaning, implies many possible referents or conceptions. Language development progresses by the child making these implied conceptions explicit through the process that has been termed here *guided reinvention*. Thus a path may be seen running from the infant's first cry to his saying, for example, "I want to go out" or "Teddy's asleep". That path leads from a general communicative ability of a natural but utterly indeterminate kind to a specific ability only applicable within a specific society; language development being located, in the theory proposed here, very much in the context in which language is used—the biological and social world.

References

Allport, F. H. (1924). *Social Psychology*. Houghton-Mifflin, Cambridge, Mass. (Cited by Greenfield, 1973).

Austin, J. L. (1962). *How to do Things with Words*. Oxford University Press, Oxford.

Bates, E. (1976). *Language and Context: the Acquisition of Pragmatics*. Academic Press, New York and London.

Bates, E., Camaioni, L. and Voltera, V. (1975). The acquisition of performatives prior to speech. *Merril-Palmer Quarterly* **21**, 205–226.

Bloom, L. (1970). *Language Development: Form and Function in Emerging Grammars*. M. I. T. Press, Cambridge, Mass.

Bloom, L. (1973). *One Word at a Time*. Mouton, The Hague.

Bowerman, M. (1973). *Early Syntactic Development: A Cross-Linguistic Study with Special Reference to Finnish*. Cambridge University Press, Cambridge.

Braine, M. D. S. (1976). Children's first word combinations. *Monogr. Soc. Res. Child Dev.* **41**.

Brown, R. (1973). *A First Language: the Early Stages*. George Allen and Unwin, London.

Bruner, J. S. (1974). The organization of early skilled action. In *The Integration of a Child into a Social World* (Ed. M. P. M. Richards). Cambridge University Press, Cambridge.

Bruner, J. S. (1976). From communication to language: a psychological perspective. *Cognition* **3** (3): 255–287.

Carpenter, E. (1966). Image making in arctic art. In *Sign, Image and Symbol* (Ed. G. Kepes) Studio Vista, London.

Chomsky, N. (1957). *Syntactic Structures*. Mouton, The Hague.

Chomsky, N. (1965). *Aspects of the Theory of Syntax*. M. I. T. Press, Cambridge, Mass.

Chomsky, N. (1968). *Language and Mind*. Harcourt, Brace and World, New York.

Cicourel, A. V. (1973). *Cognitive Sociology*. Penguin, Harmondsworth.

Clark, R. A. (1978). The transition from action to gesture. In *Action, Gesture and Symbol: The Emergence of Language* (Ed. A. J. Lock). Academic Press, New York and London.

Cohen, M. (1952). Sur l'étude du langage enfantin. *Enfance* **5**, 181–249. (cited by Greenfield and Smith, 1976).

Collingwood, R. G. (1939). *An Autobiography*. Oxford University Press, Oxford.

Cooley, C. H. (1902). *Human Nature and the Social Order*. Charles Scribner's Sons, New York.

Darwin, C. (1872). *The Expression of the Emotions in Man and Animals*. John Murray, London.

Dore, J. (1975). Holophrases, speech acts and language universals. *Journal of Child Language* **2**, 21–40.

Dore, J. (1977). Children's illocutionary acts. In *Discourse Comprehension and Production* (Ed. R. Freedle). Lawrence Erlbaum Associates, New York.

Dreyfus, H. L. (1967). Why computers must have bodies in order to be intelligent. *The Review of Metaphysics* **21**, 13–32.

Edwards, D. (1973). Sensory-motor intelligence and semantic relations in early child grammar. *Cognition* **2**, 395–434.

Feldman, H., Goldin-Meadow, S. and Gleitman, L. (1978). Beyond Herodotus: the creation of language by linguistically deprived deaf children. In *Action, Gesture and Symbol: The Emergence of Language* (Ed. A. J. Lock). Academic Press, London and New York.

Fillmore, C. J. (1968). The case for case. In *Universals in Linguistic Theory* (Eds. E. Bach and E. T. Harms). Holt, Rinehart and Winston, New York.

Flavell, J. H. (1963). *The Developmental Psychology of Jean Piaget*. D. Van Nostrand, Princeton, N. J.

Goldin-Meadow, S. and Feldman, H. (1977). The development of language-like communication without a language model. *Science* **197**, 401–403.

Gordon, D. and Lakoff, G. (1971). Conversational postulates. *Papers from the 7th Regional Meeting, Chicago Linguistic Society*, 63–84.

Greenfield, P. M. (1973). Who is "Dada?". Some aspects of the semantic and phonological development of a child's first words. *Language and Speech* **16**, 34–43.

Greenfield, P. M. and Smith, J. (1976). *The Structure of Communication in Early Language Development*. Academic Press, New York and London.

Greenfield, P. M., Smith, J. and Laufer, B. (1972). *Communication and the Beginnings of Language: The Development of Structure in One-Word Speech and Beyond*. Working Draft, Harvard University.

Grice, H. P. (1968). Utterer's meaning, sentence-meaning and word-meaning. *Foundations of Language* **4**, 1–18.

Gruber, J. S. (1967). Topicalisation in child language. *Foundations of Language* **3**, 37–65.

Guillaume, P. (1927). Les débuts de la phrase dans la langage de l'enfant. *Journal de Psychologie* **24**, 203–229.

Harré, R. and Secord, P. F. (1972). *The Explanation of Social Behaviour*. Blackwell, Oxford.

Ingram, D. (1971). Transitivity in child language. *Language* **47**, 888–910.

Ingram, D. (1975). Language development during the sensori-motor period. Paper presented at the International Child Language Symposium, London.

Ingram, D. (1978). Sensori-motor intelligence and language development. In *Action, Gesture and Symbol: The Emergence of Language* (Ed. A. J. Lock) Academic Press, London and New York.

James, W. (1965). *The Will to Believe.* Dover Books, New York.

Jesperson, O. (1922). *Language: Its Nature, Development and Origin.* George Allen and Unwin, London.

Konner, M. J. (1972). Aspects of the developmental ethology of a foraging people. In *Ethological Studies of Child Behaviour* (Ed. N. G. Burton-Jones). Cambridge University Press, Cambridge. (Cited by Richards, 1974a).

de Laguna, G. A. (1927). *Speech: Its Function and Development.* Yale University Press, New Haven.

Lakoff, R. (1972). Language in context. *Language* **48**, 907–927.

Lee, D. (1950). Codifications of reality: lineal and non-lineal. *Psychosomatic Medicine* **12**, 89–97.

Latif, I. (1934). The physiological basis of linguistic development and the ontogeny of meaning, I, II. *Psychological Review* **41**, 55–85. 153–176.

Leonard, L. B. (1976). *Meaning in Child Language.* Grune and Stratton, New York.

Leopold, W. (1939–49). *Speech Development of a Bilingual Child,* 3 vols. Northwestern Universities Press, Evanston, Ill.

Lienhardt, G. (1961). *Divinity and Experience: The Religion of the Dinka.* Clarendon Press, Oxford.

Lindsay, (Robert) of Pitscottie, (1728). *The History of Scotland from 21 February, 1436 to March, 1565, from the most authentick and most correct manuscripts. To which is added a contribution, by another hand till August, 1604* (Edited by R. Freebairn). Edinburgh.

Lock, A. J. (1976). Acts not sentences. In *Baby Talk and Infant Speech* (Eds. Y. Lebrun and W. von Raffler-Engel). Swets and Zeitlinger, Lisse.

Lock, A. J. (1978). The emergence of language. In *Action, Gesture and Symbol: The Emergence of Language* (Ed. A. J. Lock). Academic Press, London and New York.

Lukens, H. (1896). Preliminary report on the learning of language. *Pedagogical Seminary* **3**: 424–460 (Cited by Ingram. 1971).

Magee, B. (1973). *Popper.* Fontana, London.

Mead, G. H. (1912). The mechanism of social consciousness. *Journal of Philosophy* **9**, 401–406.

Mead, G. H. (1934). *Mind, Self and Society.* Chicago Universities Press, Chicago.

Moore, K. (1896). The mental development of a child. *Psychological Review: Monograph Supplements 1* (3 parts 4): 115–145.

Morehead, D. and Morehead, A. (1974). From signal to sign: a Piagetian view of thought and language during the first two years. In *Language Perspectives: Acquisition, Retardation and Intervention* (Eds. R. Schiefelbusch and L. Lloyd). University Park Press, Baltimore.

McCarthy, D. (1954). Language development in children. In *Manual of Child Psychology* (Ed. L. Carmichael). Wiley, New York.

Macfarlane, A. (1974). If a smile is so important. *New Scientist* **62** (895): 164–166.

Macfarlane, A. (1977). *The Psychology of Childbirth.* Open Books/Fontana, London.

Macmurray, J. (1961). *Persons in Relation.* Faber and Faber, London.

MacNamara, J. (1972). Cognitive basis of language learning in infants. *Psychological Review* **79**, 1–13.

McNeill, D. (1970). *The Acquisition of Language.* Harper and Row, New York.

Newson, J. (1972). Unpublished manuscript, Department of Psychology, Nottingham University.

Piaget, J. (1923). *Le Langage et la Pensée chez l'enfant.* Delachaux and Niestlé, Neuchatel and Paris. M. Gabin (trans.) *The Language and Thought of the Child.* Routledge and Kegan Paul, London: Harcourt, New York, 1926. (cited by Greenfield and Smith, 1976).

Piaget, J. (1951). *Play, Dreams and Imitation in Children.* Routledge and Kegan Paul, London.

Piaget, J. (1952). *The Origins of Intelligence in Children.* International Universities Press, New York.

Popper, K. (1972). *Objective Knowledge: An Evolutionary Approach.* Oxford University Press, Oxford.

Ramer, A. (1974). Syntactic styles and universal aspects of language emergence. Ph.D. Dissertation. City University of New York.

Ramer, A. (1975). The merging of the communicative and categorial functions of language. Paper presented to the American Speech and Hearing Association, Washington, D.C.

Richards, M. P. M. (1974). First steps in becoming social. In *The Integration of a Child into a Social World* (Ed. M. P. M. Richards). Cambridge University Press, Cambridge.

Ripin, R. (1930). A study of the infant's feeding reactions in the first six months of life. *Archives of Psychology* **116**.

Ryan, J. (1974). Early language development. In *The Integration of a Child into a Social World* (Ed. M. P. M. Richards). Cambridge University Press, Cambridge.

Sanborn, D. A. (1971). *The Language Process.* Mouton, The Hague.

Schaffer, H. R. (1977). *Studies in Mother-Infant Interaction.* Academic Press, London and New York.

Schlesinger, I. (1974). Relational concepts underlying language. In *Language Perspectives: Acquisition, Retardation, and Intervention* (Eds. R. Schiefelbush and L. Lloyd). University Park Press, Baltimore.

Searle, J. (1969). *Speech Acts.* Cambridge University Press, Cambridge.

Shotter, J. D. (1973a). Prolegomena to an understanding of play. *Journal for the Theory of Social Behaviour* **3**, 47–89.

Shotter, J. D. (1973b). Acquired powers: the transformation of natural into personal powers. *Journal for the Theory of Social Behaviour* **3**, 140–156.

Shotter, J. D. (1974a). The development of personal powers. In *The Integration of a Child into a Social World* (Ed. M. P. M. Richards). Cambridge University Press, Cambridge.

Shotter, J. D. (1974b). What is it to be human? In *Reconstructing Social Psychology* (Ed. N. Armistead). Penguin Books, Harmondsworth.

Sinclair, H. (1973). Language acquisition and cognitive development. In *Cognitive Development and the Acquisition of Language* (Ed. T. Moore). Academic Press, New York and London.

Sinclair, H. (1975). The role of cognitive structures in language acquisition. *Foundations of Language Development* (Eds. E. Lenneberg and E. Lenneberg). Academic Press, New York and London.

Slobin, D. I. (1970). Universals of grammatical development in children. In *Advances in Psycholinguistics* (Eds. G. B. Flores d'Arcais and W. M. Levelt). North Holland, Amsterdam.

Slobin, D. I. (1972). Seven questions about language development. In *New Horizons in Psychology* (Ed. P. C. Dodwell), Vol. 2. Penguin, Harmondsworth.

Smedslund, J. (1969). Meanings, implications and universals: Towards a Psychology of Man. *Scandinavian Journal of Psychology* **10**, 1–15.

Smith, J. (1970). Development and structure of holophrases. Unpublished honours thesis, Harvard University.

Spitz, R. A. (1957). *No and Yes: On the Genesis of Human Communication.* International Universities Press, New York.

Spitz, R. A. (1965). *The First Year of Life.* International Universities Press, New York.

Stern, W. (1930). The chief periods of further speech development. In *Psychology or Early Childhood* (Trans. A. Berwell). Allen and Unwin, London. Reprinted in *Child Language: A Book of Readings* (Eds. A. Bar-adon and W. Leopold). Prentice-Hall, Englewood Cliffs, N.J., 1971, pp. 45–51. (cited by Greenfield and Smith, 1976).

Strawson, P. F. (1964). Intention and convention in speech acts. *The Philosophical Review* **LXXIII**, 439–460.

Sugarman, S. (1973). A description of communicative development in the pre-language child. Unpublished honours thesis, Hampshire College, Amherst, Mass.

Vygotsky, L. S. (1962). *Thought and Language.* M. I. T. Press, Cambridge, Mass.

Vygotsky, L. S. (1966). Development of the higher mental functions. In *Psychological Research in the U.S.S.R.* Progress Publishers, Moscow.

Werner, H. and Kaplan, B. (1963). *Symbol Formation.* Wiley, New York.

Index

R

Rich interpretation,
  and gestures, 84–85
  problems of, 146
  role in language development, 173–174
  and semantic force, 84–85
  use by mother, 85, 145–146

S

Semantic force,
  and action/agent naming, 152–165
  assignment of, 83–86
  and crying, 90
  and implicatoin, 89–90, 152
  and language development, 133–134, 150–152
  and meaning, 86
  and necessary action, 89–90
  representation of, 82
  and speech acts, 81–82
  structure of, 92–94
Sensori-motor knowledge,
  and communication, 193–194
  and development of knowledge, 43–44
  and gestural development, 102–104
  and language development, 142 ff., 170
Social interaction,
  and development, 3, 42, 43–45, 57
  and goal construction, 67–79
  and learning to eat, 73–79
Social worlds, 2, 46, 47, 88, 104, 196

T

Two-word speech,
  categories of, 184–187
  relation to gesture, 180–183
  relation to one-word speech, 177–184
  and sentences, 181–183

V

Volitional utterances,
  development of, 126–129
  relation to gesture, 129
Vygotsky, L. S.,
  development of pointing, 58–59
  inter- and intramental levels, 26, 33, 46, 53
  laws of cultural development, 26, 52–53, 69
  and self concept, 189

W

Words,
  acquisition of, 108–113
  as coding knowledge, 142 ff.
  and implication, 191
  naming, development of, 113–120, 130–135
  as "pure performatives", 112
  relation to gesture, 124–126, 134–135, 179–182
World 3, 34, 122